Conserva
Moderate
Liberal

The Biblical
Authority Debate

Conservative Moderate Liberal

The Biblical Authority Debate

edited by Charles R. Blaisdell

CBP Press
St. Louis, Missouri

Scripture quotations marked RSV are from the Revised Standard Version of the Bible, copyrighted 1946, 1952, © 1971, 1973, by the Division of Christian Education of the National Council of Churches in the United States of America and are used by permission.

Quotations marked NRSV are from the New Revised Standard Version Bible, copyrighted 1989, Division of Christian Education of the National Council of Churches in the United States of America and are used by permission.

Chapter one is altered from "Contemporary Confession and Biblical Authority" by William Placher, in *To Confess the Faith Today*, edited by Jack L. Stotts and Jane Dempsey Douglass. © 1990 Jack L. Stotts and Jane Dempsey Douglass. Used by permission of Westminster/John Knox Press.

.Library of Congress Cataloging-in-Publication Data

Conservative, moderate, liberal : the biblical authority debate / edited by Charles R. Blaisdell.
    Papers presented at a conference held at Christian Theological Seminary, Sept. 27-28, 1989
    1. Bible—Evidences, authority, etc.—Congresses. I. Blaisdell, Charles R.
BS480.C624 1989   220.1'3   90-20414
ISBN 0-8272-0455-8

Printed in the United States of America

Contents

Preface

In the fall of 1989, approximately one hundred fifty people gathered at Christian Theological Seminary in Indianapolis to hear eleven speakers, representing seven different denominations or traditions, discuss the nature of biblical authority. Conversation among the presenters and with the audience was spirited, even heated at times. The conference received local and national media attention, for Independent Baptists normally do not discuss such issues with Roman Catholics, Disciples do not have much in the way of formal ecumenical relationships with Southern Baptists, and the list could be continued. What was so striking in the minds of the participants and the audience—which represented every position of the spectrum, from arch-conservative to ultra-liberal—was the very fact that such a discussion was taking place at all. When asked what the conference had accomplished, one of the presenters responded, "We all got together for two days and didn't kill each other!"

While this may seem a rather minimal criterion for evaluating the results of such an undertaking, in another sense it is not. The history of Christianity is too full of examples where even talking to the "enemy" has been deemed a sign of mortal apostasy, and civility toward those who differed on matters of faith a sign of one's own suspect faith.

On the other hand, the conference, and this volume, did not and will not usher in the kingdom of God. Serious, sometimes seemingly intractable differences remain among those who gathered. The conference neither achieved, nor was it hoped to achieve, a sort of grand synthesis that overcame all differences. One of the results of the conference, evident in this volume, is that some fundamental differences on the nature of biblical authority are *not* a result of "misunderstandings." The papers gathered here show all too well that the writers *do* understand one another, and so the fundamental differences between positions become startlingly, if troublingly, clear. The reader who is upset by Christian disunity and earnestly wishes that "they all might be one" will find that such earnestness is not match enough against these foundational differences.

It might be argued that the very structure of the conference, and of this volume, unnecessarily magnifies these differences. The three middle major papers of the conference were specifically invited to address the topic of biblical authority from "conservative," "moderate," and "liberal" positions. And each of these papers evoked responses from participants representing the other two perspectives. Such a structure indeed magnifies the differences, but not inappropriately. The differences are magnified in the sense that through such a scheme we are enabled to see them more clearly. Moreover, as Robert Wuthnow (among others) has so ably argued in *The Restructuring of American Religion,* the important dividing lines on the American Christian religious scene are no longer denominational, but ideological. William Placher begins his essay by calling into question the usefulness and appropriateness of these categories, and yet it is also clear that Christians understand (or think they understand) and use such quasi-political designations. The terms are now a ubiquitous part of the theological and ecclesial landscape. In our day, they immediately signify more—sometimes mistakenly, perhaps—than do denominational tags. Every major American denomination currently seems to house an ongoing battle between those who are "liberal," those who are "conservative," and those who are somewhere in between. While it may be unhelpful and even unfaithful to describe faith in terms of political analogues, it is nonetheless a trend that is increasing even as the substantive doctrinal differences between "mainstream" Protestants seem to be decreasing.

William Placher opens the debate not only by questioning the appropriateness of the "liberal-moderate-conservative" schema, but by suggesting that *authority* is not a univocal term. We are tempted, he says, to think of authority as quantitative. On such a view, our immediate question, when faced with a claim to authority, is to ask, "*How much* authority?" Allied with this tendency is a view about the nature of language in which the claims of the Bible are to be understood as "propositions." To the degree the propositions match reality, they are authoritative. But there is the rub: Some "propositions," some claims in the Bible, seem to us to be morally incredible or intellectually archaic. If we fail to confer authority on these, how do we know how much authority the other claims have?

But Placher believes that we are misled by the quantitative assumption. Prior to asking about "how much" authority this or that portion of the Bible has, we ought first to ask the more phenomenological question of how does the Bible *function* as authority. It turns out that the Bible functions authoritatively in the lives of people in several different and sometimes incommensurable ways. Thus the quantitative question is a false start.

Drawing on David Kelsey's *The Uses of Scripture in Recent Theology*, Placher identifies two additional ways in which scripture functions as authority. First, it does so in that it is a "transforming word" in the lives of some. In other words, scripture's authority is discerned in how it changes lives. Citing the examples of Augustine and Schweitzer, Placher says here that scripture's authority is validated wherever the encounter with it "enables us to live human life as it is meant to be lived."

Scripture can also function as authority when it is understood and encountered as "the narration of God's identity." Here, the question is not whether this or that proposition is true, but whether scripture, considered almost as an "extended anecdote," tells the truth about what God is like. Although Placher does not put it this way, such a view of authority is predicated on a very Aristotelian notion of truth. For Aristotle, a story that might not be "true" in each of its details might nonetheless be "more true" in its portrayal of its subject than any mere assemblage of propositions might be. Poetry, for Aristotle, is more true than history because it tells the truth about the way things generally are, even if the story matches no actual set of particulars. A "story" can sometimes tell more truth about a person's character than can a biographical summary.

Underlying Jack Cottrell's "conservative" presentation, however, is an unstated question in response to Placher's second and third models of the authority of scripture: Epistemologically speaking, how do you *know* that the way that scripture has transformed someone's life is in fact "human life as it is meant to be"; or, alternatively, how do you *know* that scripture is indeed "telling the truth" about God? Throughout his paper, Cottrell is clear about the nature of the problem. Anything other than the propositional model entails that something other than scripture must serve as the criterion for *recognizing* truth or truthfulness. But to allow anything other than the propositional model, he believes, is to be ineluctably drawn into an epistemological relativism wherein you may have the truth—but you can never know that you know.

Cottrell argues instead that scripture's authority must be understood propositionally. Scripture indeed may transform, it may indeed narrate identity, but it does so truthfully because it is anchored in propositional claims that can in principle be verified. And where such claims of scripture cannot be verified—the fundamental assertions about the *nature* of Christ's life and death, for example—then they are authoritative because they issue from someone we trust: God. Scripture is authoritative because it expresses the mind of God, the very words of God. Where the Bible transforms lives, or where it has powerful emotional or spiritual effect on people, those experiences cannot function as the index of truth. Rather, the experiences themselves must be judged in relation to the self-certifying words of God as expressed in scripture.

Cottrell's respondents, Gloria Tate and Barbara Blaisdell, raise questions with Cottrell's view. "Moderate" Tate believes that such a propositional, word-revelational view of scripture does not allow for any authoritative contemporary workings of the Holy Spirit. Moreover, says Tate, it is a mistake to think that human language, beset with problems of translation and cross-cultural diversity, can "contain the infinite." The language of scripture is time- and culture-bound and therefore inevitably skews the truth about God.

Blaisdell's response to the epistemological dilemma underlying Cottrell's position is to argue that if Cottrell's propositional view is correct, then the Bible tells us things about God, and counsels us to do things, that are morally offensive, intellectually implausible, or unintelligible. One must approach the Bible, in her view, with an awareness of the deepest intuitions about what is good. One reads the Bible with a critical correlation in mind between what it claims and what such intuitions, discerned as carefully and as humbly as possible, would tell us. Cottrell's word-revelational schema (and his verificationist views about how language works) "does not admit full room for moral reflection or coherence or plausibility with our experience." Under his view, she xii

writes, "Reason has no authority. It *does not* allow the questions, 'Is this teaching moral?' or 'Does this make any sense?'" Yet, "we must ask these questions of *every* claim to truth." David Scholer's "moderate" presentation might be described as an attempt to retain the conviction that the Bible can be understood to be completely authoritative, and yet is also inescapably marked by the cultural particularities of its writers. Scholer believes that evangelicals have always had a difficult time acknowledging the real historicity of the biblical texts, a kind of biblical docetism. Thus, he rejects inerrancy, for he believes that inerrancy confuses the issues of biblical authority and biblical interpretation. In fact, inerrancy's commitment is to "a larger philosophical framework that is not true to experience." For "experience makes it clear that a completely rational, ordered universe as a conceptual framework is not possible; there are inconsistencies and irreconcilable data." The inerrantist position raises the stakes in such a way that if there is one "error, or even one perceived variance," everything about God is thereby questionable.

In Scholer's view, the Bible is authoritative because it is informed by the Spirit of God, and its principle of unity is precisely in its very diversity. Instead of either eliminating contradictory texts, or going to sometimes strained efforts to harmonize them, we should find the Bible's "total beautiful unity by its very diversity." And, "we must let the Bible gloriously speak; and part of its 'glory' consists in its multifaceted diversity."

In Richard Land's "conservative" response to Scholer, he argues that the consensus view of scripture, throughout the history of the church, has in fact been the view that has been labeled in the last century as "inerrancy." Citing the work of Mark Noll, Land believes that "for most Christians, in most places, in most traditions, at most times, the Bible has been understood and accepted as 'entirely truthful.'" Such a view is supported by the "overwhelming preponderance of the evidence." Yet Land realizes that such a descriptive assertion does not answer the normative question of whether such an assessment of the Bible is correct.

Against Scholer, Land argues that the cultural particularity and historicity of biblical texts does not call into question their inerrancy. One can easily maintain that the authors of the texts were completely inspired by God, just as were their various historical/psychological peculiarities. Shifting away from Scholer's quilt metaphor, Land says that scripture can be likened to a stained glass mosaic, through which we see the light—but the "glass" itself (with its apparent imperfections) is also designed by God. Thus, "the individual mosaics that are the human aspects and facets of the biblical writers are the individual, differently tinted hues that compose the design God wanted us to see."

Land also argues that those groups or traditions that have abandoned this sort of view of the Bible find themselves in trouble: "When one looks at the historical record, one finds that those who have abandoned a high view of scripture...have far more often than not found it very difficult to sustain a high view of authority and doctrinal orthodoxy." Yet Land realizes that such is an argument from consequences and is merely suggestive rather than compelling. Conversely, "the success and vitality of evangelicalism...finds one of its most important sources in the certainty that it carries...a sure and a certain word from God."

Charles Allen's "liberal" response to Scholer focuses on the hermeneutical and ethical problems attendant on seeing the scriptures as diverse in their messages and their historical situations. For such diversity entails "tensions" in the biblical witness, and while many such tensions may indeed be "fruitful," Allen writes, "I cannot find a fruitful tension between testimonies to God's unconditional love and portrayals of God commanding acts of genocide."

Rather than simply accepting such tensions, as Scholer seems to counsel, Allen suggests that interpreters of the Bible see themselves as integral parts of the traditioning process that can be seen in the canon itself. "As a liberal," he writes, "if I identify some portion or theme of scripture as hopelessly disordered, I do not pretend to stand above scripture's traditioning process. I am instead playing a minor part in that very same process." For "just as I confess Jesus as the Christ because I finally cannot help myself, so do I also frequently find myself unable to keep from acknowledging that there is much in scripture that runs counter to that confession." Allen anticipates the theme found in Luke Johnson's "liberal" presentation, that the New Testament itself authorizes its interpreters to exercise the *exousia* of entering "into a conversation with these diverse views and opinions expressed by the New Testament, finding in their areas of overlap as well as in their points of divergence guidance for our own decisions." Johnson's warrant for this view is that the New Testament writers themselves were playing the very same role, and exercising the very same *exousia*, in regard to the Torah. What is the limit of such interpretive authority? It "will be set by the integrity of the individual and community identity as measured by the messianic pattern authored by these same writings."

Johnson believes that the authority of the New Testament is a several-sided affair. The New Testament is not concerned solely with doctrinal orthodoxy; it is concerned with fostering a certain specific type of community *identity*. In fact, it is here, rather than in the "thematic jumble" of beliefs and practices attested to in the New Testament, wherein we find the "greatest degree of unanimity within the variety of [the New Testament's] literary forms and distinctive authorial perspectives." All the New Testament writings "converge on the matter of identity: the meaning of life before God in light of a crucified and raised Messiah whose Spirit enlivens a character expressed by faith, hope, and love....Here is where the New Testament is most reliable and trustworthy."

John Hosler's "conservative" response to Johnson disputes the view that the New Testament authorizes its interpreters to participate in the very same *exousia* regarding "doctrine" as did its writers. Citing a number of examples from the early church fathers, Hosler maintains that in fact the earliest interpreters of the New Testament regarded the doctrines given there as fixed and sufficient. The apostolic provenance of the writings assures that there is nothing further that human interpreters need to supply. "I attempt to require," Hosler writes, "that none of my Christian doctrines will have originated with myself or my denomination. They must have originated with Christ and have been delivered to the church via the original apostles and through the scriptures." This is the "doctrinal *exousia* chain of command." Otherwise, Hosler says, "I would be attempting to limit God if I proclaimed that He is incapable of placing scriptural boundaries on what He will allow us to know about His will for mankind."

George Tooze's "moderate" response to Johnson is meditative in quality. He raises a number of questions with Johnson, as well as citing several areas of agreement. He notes, for example, that Johnson's midrashic model takes no account of how to deal with the non-Torah portions of the Hebrew scriptures. He also believes that Johnson underestimates the importance of the Bible's authority as a symbol. Whereas Johnson labels some such uses as "talismanic," Tooze believes that "the Bible as a symbol [can] bring an authoritative Word from the God whom it represents to a number of places." And, Tooze writes, "in the end, I do not have a clear sense of exactly where Johnson ultimately places his sense of authority." If the New Testament authorizes in its readers interpretive *exousia*, "if it is in the *process* that authority is found, then I am concerned for its subjectivity, for process is subjective and really can move in any direction the winds will take it."

In its way, Tooze's argument is akin to Land's argument from consequences: People want and need "a word of hope and of faith that would give them the courage to meet the needs of each day." Therefore, "on a practical basis...I need to assume the Spirit of God inherent in...[the scripture], and I have to assume that under the guidance of the Holy Spirit that Word has authority to shape and mold my life." We must make this assumption, says Tooze, based on the religious and existential needs of people; that need is the starting point for how one views the New Testament.

The closing essay in this volume, Edgar Towne's "The Future of Biblical Authority," raises the question in phenomenological terms of why there are such differing views of the authority of the Bible. Arguing from a phenomenological aesthetics, Towne says that "our respect and use of the Bible can be said to involve an aesthetic object...created by the interplay of text and interpreter." There is a transaction between the text's "encoded meaning" and all of the interpreter's beliefs. Moreover, such beliefs are multi-faceted, impinging on every aspect of life, and all of them are brought to any encounter with a text. It is therefore no wonder that the theological construals of such aesthetic experiences vary. Each interpreter's encounter with a biblical text is absolutely unique in content, given the interplay between text and the particular interpreter. The unity to be found in the Bible, Towne seems to be saying, is actually to be found in the aesthetic structure of experience which is the same formally for everyone, but which materially will always differ. This accounts for the apparent intractability of the discussion of theological construals of biblical authority. Yet, perhaps this "can help us appreciate how the grace of the Holy Spirit creates and preserves our unity despite our interpretive differences."

I would like to thank a number of persons for their assistance with this volume. Professors Ronald Allen and Edgar Towne, of the Christian Theological Seminary faculty, provided invaluable assistance and counsel concerning the shape of both the conference and this volume. Nor would either this book or the conference have been possible without the support of the Lilly Endowment, whose grant to Christian Theological Seminary has helped further such conversations across theological lines. This volume could not have been produced without the gracious assistance of Kathleen Bell and Karen Kelm; they managed to type and retype this manuscript under the pressures of the opening of a semester.

A note: Many readers will find in these papers pronominal and other references that seem inappropriate. Rather than change the words of the individual writers where they have used references to "mankind," and to God as "he," I have allowed their language to stand, believing that this approach renders their positions as clear as they would wish.

Charles R. Blaisdell

Contributors

Charles Allen is instructor of religion at Marian College and Indiana University-Purdue University, Indianapolis. Formerly the director of the Project on Evaluation in Religious Studies for the Lilly Endowment, he has his Ph.D. from the University of Chicago and is the author of several published articles.

Barbara Blaisdell is senior minister of Central Christian Church, Indianapolis. She is an M.Div. graduate of Christian Theological University, has taught for Vincennes University, and is the author of several articles published in *Encounter*. She has served pastorates in Indiana and Texas.

Charles Blaisdell is assistant to the president, Christian Theological Seminary, Indianapolis, and adjunct instructor of philosophy at the University of Indianapolis. A graduate of Christian Theological Seminary, Vanderbilt University, and the University of Chicago, he has taught at Vanderbilt and Butler Universities. He is the author of a number of articles published in *Encounter, Process Studies,* etc. He has served pastorates in Indiana and Texas.

Jack Cottrell teaches at the Cincinnati Bible College and Seminary. His Ph.D. is from Princeton University and he is the author of *What the Bible Says About God* and *Tough Questions/Biblical Answers*. He has served pastorates in Indiana, Ohio, Kentucky, and Pennsylvania.

John Hosler is the pastor of Lifegate Baptist Church, Indianapolis, and teaches at Martin Center College, Indianapolis. He has also taught at Midwest Bible College and Baptist Bible College of Indianapolis and has served pastorates in Indiana and Illinois. He is the author of *Perspectives on the First Amendment*.

Luke Johnson is professor of New Testament and Christian Origins at Indiana University. He received his Ph.D. from Yale University and taught there from 1976 to 1982. He is the author of *The Writings of the New Testament* and *Decision Making in the Church.*

Richard Land is the executive director of the Christian Life Commission of the Southern Baptist Convention. A graduate of Princeton and Oxford Universities, he has taught and been vice-president for academic affairs at Criswell College. He has served pastorates in Texas, Louisiana, and England, and has been the assistant to the governor of the state of Texas.

William Placher teaches religion at Wabash College. His Ph.D. is from Yale University and he is the author of *A History of Christian Thought* and *Unapologetic Theology.* He has taught at Haverford College, been a visiting scholar at Stanford University, and a fellow of the Center for Theological Inquiry at Princeton University.

David Scholer teaches New Testament and Early Christian History at North Park College and Seminary, Chicago. A graduate of Gordon Divinity School and Harvard, he has taught at Gordon-Conwell Theological Seminary and Northern Baptist Seminary. He is the author of numerous articles on biblical interpretation and women's ministry.

Gloria Tate is the pastor of Immanuel Presbyterian Church, Indianapolis, where she has served for thirteen years. A graduate of Coe College and Johnson Smith Seminary, she has served pastorates in Georgia and South Carolina and has served as co-chair of the National Council of Churches Women's Caucus.

George Tooze is senior minister of First Baptist Church, Indianapolis. He is a graduate of Gordon College and Seminary, as well as Andover-Newton Theological Seminary. He has served pastorates in Massachusetts and is the author of a bibliography published on Emily Judson.

Edgar Towne is professor of theology at Christian Theological Seminary, Indianapolis. A Ph.D. graduate of the University of Chicago, he has served pastorates in West Virginia and Illinois and has taught at Findlay College, Ohio. He is the author of several articles.

1

The Nature of Biblical Authority: Issues and Models from Recent Theology

William C. Placher

Let me begin subversively. When we think about biblical authority in contemporary America, our natural tendency is to treat the issue as a multiple-choice question and rank all the answers on a single continuum. The titles of the subsequent contributions to this volume risk suggesting such an approach. A "conservative" perspective. "Moderate." "Liberal." The very terms hint of measuring and ranking degrees of authority. The words—and I suspect this is significant—come originally from the language of politics, not of religion. One of them even acquired a measure of notoriety in the last presidential campaign: the "l-word." No doubt a deconstructionist critic would make much of the punctuation of our original lecture titles, where quotation marks abound. Even as we use these labels, we are not quite comfortable with them.

I have begun my attempt at subversion with irony, but my intent is a serious one. The continued use of such essentially political terms embodies some deep mistakes. It is dangerous to continue to think that the only question to ask about the authority of scripture is "how much authority?" The danger afflicts not only our intellectual clarity but the very health of Christ's church. I want to suggest some different questions and perhaps even some new answers. In particular, I will argue that there are different ways of thinking about the Bible as authoritative that we cannot rank on a single scale—not less authority or more, but just different, functioning as authority in different ways. I will explore three such models of scriptural authority in this essay.

Professor Robert Wuthnow of Princeton University recently published an important book entitled *The Restructuring of American Religion*. One of his theses is that the key dividing lines in American Christianity have changed. A generation ago, denominational lines mattered most. In 1949 the Episcopal Church passed a resolution warning its members against marrying Roman Catholics. A few years later the General Assembly of the Presbyterian Church (USA) officially condemned the "cultic worship of Mary" among Catholics. In 1946 the prominent fundamentalist writer Ernest Gordon had written, "In many cities Roman churches are nests of bingo gambling and, in the Whiskey Trust, Vatican investments are very large indeed. Back of the corrupt city machines are the Roman hierarchies."[1] On the other side, in 1947 Francis Cardinal Spellman dismissed Protestant critics of Catholicism as "unhooded klansmen."[2] Divisions among Protestant denominations were less sharp, but in their classic sociological study of an American community, Robert and Helen Lynd concluded that most of the residents of their "Middletown"—Muncie, Indiana, in the 1920s—had been reared in a single denomination, seldom switched to another, and knew very little about the beliefs and practices of other denominations.[3] Wuthnow makes a good case that that pattern had not changed overmuch by the 1950s or even 60s.

It is hard to believe that I have been describing American Christianity as it existed within our lifetimes. We live today in such a different world. In our ecumenical age, Protestants and Catholics, let alone Methodists and Presbyterians and Lutherans and Disciples of Christ, rarely attack each other in either national statements or sermons in the local churches. Indeed, one of the great concerns I hear from pastors in my own Presbyterian denomination—and I am sure we are not unique—is that most of the people in their congregations were not reared as Presbyterians and do not know what it means to be a Presbyterian. At least among most Protestant bodies, denominational loyalties just mean less and less.

It does not follow that American Christians have all become one big happy family. You will have a hard time finding an anti-Catholic or anti-Protestant or anti-Lutheran or anti-Presbyterian sermon these days. On the other hand, attacks on "fundamentalists" or "TV evangelists," or, from a different perspective, "liberals" or "secular humanists," are one of the staples of the contemporary American pulpit. On the Catholic side the issues are different, but Catholics self-consciously in the tradition of Vatican II may find they have more in common with liberal Protestants than with their conservative Catholic brothers and sisters, while more conservative Catholics looking for allies on issues from abortion to women's ordination may turn most naturally to evangelical Protestants. In short, Wuthnow's carefully documented thesis corresponds to our own experience: The lines we draw between "us" and "them" these days, the differences that really matter, are often those defined by labels like fundamentalists, evangelicals, conservatives, liberals, moderates, mainline.

The authority of the Bible often seems the crucial issue on which these lines are drawn. It is therefore appropriately with such categories that we begin. Yet, as I have said, these categories make me nervous. To explain why, let me shift my discourse from the sociological to the confessional: I do not find myself comfortable with any of those labels when applied to me. I suspect my experience is a common one, so let me try to describe it.

4

Many of the values and assumptions of contemporary American society seem to me deeply flawed. Too many of our children turn to drugs. In our cities the homeless wander the streets in the shadow of great wealth. We continue to build the weaponry that may destroy us all, if ecological catastrophe does not hit first. The list of crises is a familiar one. Incarnate symbols of greed seem too often our heroes, and both our national leaders and the majority of the public at large seem more upset about flag burnings than about cross burnings in the front yards of black families or one of the highest rates of infant mortality in the industrialized world.

As a Christian, particularly in that context, I find myself seized by the power of the Bible, with its radically different vision of how things are and ought to be. Not the millionaire, not the movie star, not the basketball coach, not the president, but this carpenter's son executed by the authorities of his time offers the model of the most fully human life. Not greed, not lust, not ambition for power, but awe at the omnipotence and grace of God and love for even the least of our sisters and brothers are the virtues we ought to cultivate.

If someone says that none of that fits with the prevailing beliefs of our society, then so much the worse for the prevailing beliefs of our society. In the words of that heroic Christian confession of faith in the face of Nazi tyranny, the Barmen Declaration, "We reject the false doctrine, as though the Church were permitted to abandon the form of its message and order to its own pleasure or to changes in prevailing ideological and political convictions."[4] The Bible calls us to a different vision of things, discrepant to the dominant ethos of our culture, and, compelled by it, we can only say of scripture what the crowd in Galilee said of our Lord so long ago: It teaches as one who has authority.

On the other hand, there are parts of the Bible I simply find very hard to believe. No doubt Rudolf Bultmann over-simplified the issue in his famous remark, "We cannot use electric lights and radios and in the event of illness avail ourselves of modern medical and clinical means and at the same time believe in the spirit and wonder world of the New

Testament."⁵ Yet when we read of the multiplication of loaves and fishes, walking on water, casting out demons, do not many of us find ourselves at a loss, struggling or unable to believe, wondering if we have to believe, wondering just what we are called to believe?

Perhaps more seriously, we read the negative references to "the Jews" in John's gospel and remember the whole tragic history of Christian anti-Semitism. Christian men hear the pain in many women's voices as they talk about how the male language of parts of scripture and the passages that explicitly cast women in a subordinate role evoke for them the whole history of the oppression of women in the Jewish and Christian traditions. To put the question in strongest terms: With those memories behind us and that pain still with us, is it morally acceptable to say, unapologetically and unqualifiedly, that we must strive more fully to submit ourselves to the authority of scripture?

To put the matter bluntly, the Bible often makes us uncomfortable. Sometimes we recognize that that's good for us, that we need to let its challenge shock us out of our accustomed ways. But at other points we struggle to distinguish between the true scandal of the cross and the false scandals of the sacrifice of the intellect. I find myself, at any rate, full of such ambivalence, and so in the face of the question, "How much authority do you think the Bible has?" all the answers seem too simple. In some ways, I want to say, it has powerful authority, but in other ways I do not accept it uncritically.

If the answers seem too simple, perhaps the question is too simple. Before we ask "How much authority?" maybe we should inquire just how scripture *functions as* authority. It turns out that it can do so in a number of different ways, and that therefore we cannot measure people's views of the authority of the Bible on a single scale. In exploring these issues, let me begin by paying tribute to David Kelsey's book, *The Uses of Scripture in Recent Theology*,⁶ the best analysis we have of this topic. In what follows, I owe much to Kelsey's insights, though I lack the space to lay out his full typology, in which scripture functions as authority for theology in at least seven different ways. For our purposes, I think three general types suffice, and so I want to talk about the authority of scripture (1) as a set of true propositions, (2) as a transforming word, and (3) as the narrative of God's identity.

1. First, there is the understanding of scripture as a body of authoritative propositions. "The Bible," Charles Hodge wrote over a century ago in the greatest formulation of Princeton orthodoxy, "is to the theologian what nature is to the man of science. It is his storehouse of facts."[7] "Inspiration extends to all the contents....It is not confined to moral and religious truths, but extends to the statement of facts, whether scientific, historical, or geographical....It extends to everything which any sacred writer asserts to be true."[8] The Bible is, to use terms that may or may not mean the same thing, "verbally inspired," "infallible," "inerrant."

To conflate all those terms, and to summarize this view in the way that I have, is to caricature and distort. Hodge himself rejected the "mechanical theory of inspiration" and insisted that the prophets "were not like calculating machines which grind out logarithms with infallible correctness."[9] He distinguished *opinions* the biblical authors may have had, on a variety of topics, from what they *taught*, and he judged that only the latter is authoritative. So, for instance, the author of the book of Joshua evidently *believed* that the sun moves around the earth, and he *assumed* that when he wrote, but he did not *teach* it, and therefore it is not infallibly true and not authoritative for Christian faith.[10]

A contemporary evangelical scholar like Clark Pinnock has a similarly complex position. It is clear, he writes, "why the question of biblical authority is so important to evangelicals: belief in the infallibility of the scriptures is the pillar which supports our theology—without it the edifice would surely crumble."[11] But a few pages later, he explains that in interpreting that infallible text,

I have to take care to be more discriminating than evangelicals sometimes are. I have to take a close look at the text in its original context, observe its scope and direction, consider the question it may be answering, and the like. I must consider the strength of its affirmation, its place within the cumulative biblical revelation, and its distinctive tone within the symphony of the scriptural choir.[12]

Take all those qualifications seriously and, in practice, belief in biblical infallibility leaves a good bit of room for maneuvering. But the basic model, I think, remains clear: There are propositions in the Bible—which are true, and we accept the authority of scripture when we accept their truth.

2. Consider now a different model of scriptural authority: the model of the transforming word. Remember how in the third century St. Antony heard a sermon on the text, "If you would be perfect, go, sell what you possess and give to the poor, and you will have treasure in heaven." So he went and sold, and spent the next seventy years or so of his life in prayer and fasting in the desert.[13] We do not know anything about Antony's doctrine of biblical authority. His biographer emphasizes the hatred he bore books and schoolwork from earliest childhood,[14] and he lived in third-century Egypt, with its tradition of allegorical interpretation. So it seems unlikely that Antony spent his time poring over the literal meaning of texts. But we do not know. My point is that, in the face of Antony's life, we do not need to know his hermeneutical theory to know that for him scripture was authoritative: It transformed him, forever.

In the case of St. Augustine, we know much more, for we have his own account. Sitting in a garden in Milan, he tells us, he heard a voice repeating in a kind of singsong, "Take it and read. Take it and read." The story of Antony crossed his mind. And then:

> I rose to my feet. I snatched up the book, opened it, and read in silence the passage upon which my eyes first fell: *Not in rioting and drunkenness, not in chambering and wantonness, not in strife and envying: but put ye on the Lord Jesus Christ, and make not provision for the*

8

flesh in concupiscence. I had no wish to read further; there was no need to. For immediately I had reached the end of this sentence it was as though my heart was filled with a light of confidence and all the shadows of my doubt were swept away.[15]

Here too, all other considerations aside, the Bible is functioning authoritatively by transforming his life. Our own century has provided the interesting case of Albert Schweitzer. With Schweitzer we know, because he told us, that he did not believe the truth of many of the propositions in the Bible. Either we can know nothing at all about the teaching of Jesus, he concluded in *The Quest of the Historical Jesus,* or else at the center of that teaching stood the expectation that the world was about to end within one generation, and Jesus was simply wrong. Not a very positive account, one might think, of scriptural authority. And yet the author of that book was also Doctor Schweitzer of Lambarene, who gave up his brilliant scholarship and his career as one of the century's greatest interpreters of Bach's organ works to spend well over half his lifetime as a medical missionary in Africa. However cynical one may be about his paternalism and his attitudes toward Africa and Africans, still, there he was, year after year, tending the sick and dying. Whether the influence that the Bible had on his life—or on Augustine's or Antony's or Charles Hodge's or anyone else's—was on balance for good or for ill is a topic for another time. All I want to say here is that one cannot deny the fact that it functioned with authority for him. Jesus comes to us, he wrote in the haunting final paragraph of *The Quest,*

as One unknown, without a name, as of old, by the lake-side, He came to those men who knew Him not. He speaks to us the same word: "Follow thou me!" and sets us to the tasks which He has to fulfill for our time. He commands. And to those who obey Him, whether they be wise or simple, He will reveal Himself in the toils, the conflicts, the sufferings which they shall pass through in His fellowship, and, as an ineffable mystery, they shall learn in their own experience Who He is.[16]

It is hard to imagine a clearer case of authority that transforms life, an authority initiated in an encounter with Jesus as mediated through scripture—and yet it is hard to imagine a case where the propositional truth claims involved would be more difficult to pin down.

While it is perhaps as skeptic that Bultmann is now most widely remembered in many theological circles—the man who said we cannot know much at all about the historical Jesus, that we have to demythologize New Testament texts, pry away that husk of first-century myth that envelops them—but there is another side to Bultmann. He repeatedly affirmed that the life of authentic faith is the solution to the riddle of human existence, and that authentic faith is possible only as a result of, and in response to, the action of God in Jesus Christ. "Faith only became possible at a definite point in history in consequence of an *event*—viz., the event of Christ. Faith in the sense of obedient self-commitment and inward detachment from the world is only possible when it is faith in Jesus Christ."[17]

Now that is, in its way, a strong doctrine of the authority of scripture. The *kerygma* encounters us only through scripture, and only that *kerygma* enables us to live human life as it is meant to be lived. If you try to buttress the authority of that *kerygma* with evidence, say, for the historical accuracy of scripture, then Bultmann will insist that you are only weakening faith. "The man who wishes to believe in God as his God must realize that he has nothing in his hand on which to base his faith. He is suspended in mid-air, and cannot demand a proof of the Word which addresses him."[18] You hear the Word, and it changes your life. It speaks with authority.

A generation of theologians influenced by existentialism shared Bultmann's conviction that appeal to supporting evidence would destroy the authenticity of faith. Faith has to involve risk and courage, Paul Tillich wrote. It entails not the certitude of proof but an existential certitude that seizes one's whole existence.[19] If you say, "But look here, we have evidence for the miracles, and over five hundred witnesses for the resurrection," then you have missed the point of what it means to have Christian faith. Faith, in Soren Kierkegaard's words,

> cannot be distilled from even the nicest accuracy of detail....If the contemporary generation had left nothing behind them but these words: "We have believed that in such and such a year the God appeared among us in the humble figure of a servant, that he lived and taught in our community, and finally died," it would be more than enough...for this little advertisement...would be sufficient to afford an occasion for a successor, and the most voluminous account can in all eternity do nothing more.[20]

Contemporary liberation theologians differ from theologians influenced by existentialism in many ways—to cite the most obvious, in their greater emphasis on social and political dimensions. But I think they share a similar sense of the authority of scripture as residing in its transforming power. Thus, for instance, James Cone notes, "Black people in America had great confidence in the holy Book. This confidence has not been shaken by the rise of historical criticism." "This does not mean," he goes on to explain,

> that black people are fundamentalists in the strict sense of the term. They have not been preoccupied with definitions of inspiration and infallibility....It is as if blacks have intuitively drawn the all-important distinction between infallibility and reliability. They have not contended for a fully explicit infallibility, feeling perhaps that there is mystery in the Book, as there is in the Christ. What they have testified to is the Book's reliability: how it is the true and basic source for discovering the truth of Jesus Christ....The authority of the Bible for Christology, therefore, does not

lie in its objective status as the literal Word of God.
Rather, it is found in its power to point to the One
whom the people have met in the historical struggle
of freedom....Through the reading of scripture...they
are taken from the present to the past and then thrust
back into their contemporary history with divine
power to transform the sociopolitical context.[21]

In empowering oppressed people—in this case, African
Americans—to transform their world, the Bible speaks with
an authority that stands apart from claims about the truth of
its every proposition. It functions as authority differently
than it does on other models—not necessarily more or less,
just different.
    3. Third, one can understand the Bible as the narration of
God's identity. This view owes much to the theology of Karl
Barth, particularly as that was developed by Hans Frei—
before his recent and untimely death—into something his
Yale colleague George Lindbeck christened "postliberal
theology."[22] But it also connects with the literary analysis of
the Bible. To explain it, let me begin with a simple story. Back
in the days when Babe Ruth was a star for the New York
Yankees, one day he visited a sick boy in the hospital. To
cheer the boy up, he promised to hit a home run just for him
the next day and to announce that he was going to do it.
Comes next day's game. First time up the Babe strikes out.
Second time, a single. Third time, out on a short fly to right.
Ninth inning, Yankees behind by one, one man on base,
Ruth's last chance—and with his bat he points to the outfield
fence and then hits the next ball just where he pointed.
    Now I do not know if that story is true. I can, however,
imagine an old friend of Ruth's or a dedicated student of that
baseball era saying something like this: "I'm not sure if that
particular incident really happened, but I can tell you this.
The story captures something true about Babe Ruth's character—about his affection for kids, his arrogance, his humor, his
wildness—and about that whole crazy time in America. If
you didn't live through the twenties, and you never knew

Babe, then you learn something that's right about him and about those years from that story, something I wouldn't know how else to put into words. No set of adjectives or descriptive categories would fully capture it."

On my third model, then, the Bible as a narration of God's identity, we could take scripture as a kind of extended anecdote that tells us about God. Maybe each gospel story is not historically true, for instance, but together they make up an authentic portrait of Jesus more truthful than any attempt to translate them out of their narratives into descriptive adjectives could be.[23] Hans Frei's work drew both on the theology of Karl Barth and on literary analyses to scripture to develop such an approach, which seemed to him most faithful to the meaning of the text. As we read the gospel narratives, Frei said, we can be struck by their general casualness in matters of detail. Reading the gospels and comparing them one with another, the chronologies and the geography do not even seem consistent, and one senses that the authors did not much worry about such inconsistencies. Such specifics do not seem the subject-matter, die Sache as the Germans would say, of these texts.[24]

On the other hand, suppose someone says, "The point of these stories is simply to draw general lessons about how human life should be lived. Whether there really was a person named Jesus, and what sort of person he was, does not matter to the meaning of the gospel narratives." That seems wrong somehow. The gospels may appear indifferent to some kinds of detail, but they seem to be telling us about a unique, unsubstitutable person, Jesus of Nazareth, and claiming that who he was and what he did make all the difference to who we are and what we can hope. Their authority, therefore, resides in their witness to a person, the written word functioning as word of God in its witness to the Word of God incarnate—just as the Old Testament provides a narrative that delineates the identity of the God of Israel, the God made more fully known in Jesus Christ, the God we worship.

If one reads the Bible as this kind of narration of God's identity, then, in contrast to the propositional view, one need not worry about the historical accuracy of the details. Long stretches of biblical narrative might go by without a single historically true proposition, and yet that would not matter for Christian faith. It is not that we would want to discard those passages or dismiss them as unimportant—what matters is the portrait they convey. On the other hand, for the transforming-word model, particularly in its existentialist form, the authority of scripture lies in the individual passage that seizes our attention. For this narration-of-identity model, the narrative shape of the story as a whole becomes more important, and thus this style of biblical interpretation draws on the resources of literary analyses of scripture. Reading the Bible, we no longer take particular pericopes and ask, "Is this true?" or "What does this passage say to my life?" We now ask questions about the dramatic development of the story, the narrative flow, the insight it provides, into the mystery of personal character. Just as with a vivid anecdote, we conclude that no non-narrative translation would convey without loss all that we learn from this story. The telling of the story does not vouch for the truth of its details—as I said, the gospels seem often casual about such matters—but it invites us to see the world in the terms it uses and enter into relationship with the God it describes.[25] It is not that a particular passage provides the occasion for seizing us and transforming our lives but that the language and narrative world of the Bible as a whole come to provide a framework within which we understand our own lives as they are and might become. We accept this biblical world, with all its inconsistencies and ambiguities, as the world in which we live. When that happens, we are acknowledging the authority of scripture. Indeed, if the *meaning* of the Bible lies first of all in its narration of God's identity, then it is in doing this that we are *most* faithful to its authority.

I have set out three ways of interpreting the Bible as authority: It contains true propositions, it transforms one's life, it narrates God's identity. I am not now going to cast a strong vote for one of the three. My first conclusion harkens back to my introductory remarks. Different people find the

Bible powerfully authoritative, functioning in different ways. If there are at least these three ways of understanding the authority of scripture, then we cannot simply rank people on one scale as to how much authority they give scripture. My second conclusion would be that each of these three approaches has something to learn from the others.

It seems to me that those who focus on the authority of scripture as consisting in its true propositions risk living in a state of chronic anxiety. No one really fits the caricature of a complete biblical literalist. Everyone recognizes at least that propositions have to be understood in context, that sometimes scripture does speak in metaphor and symbol, and so forth. But if your only model for scriptural authority is a propositional one, then every such recognition can feel like a concession, an admission of partial defeat. Propositionalists are, of all of us, the most apt to fall into thinking that there is only one scale on which to rank people from most to least accepting of biblical authority. Acknowledging the complexity of the biblical texts, therefore, can feel and sound like taking them as less authoritative. The recognition that there are different ways in which scripture can function powerfully as authority might be, for such folk, liberating—even if they retain a primary allegiance to their own model of biblical interpretation.

Those who encounter scripture primarily as a transforming word also have something to learn from the other two models. The gospel transforms us authentically only because it tells us something true. It is only because God has acted that we can appropriately respond. Otherwise we would be claiming to save ourselves rather than trusting in God's grace. Moreover, I fear that that little scrap of paper with one sentence on it that Kierkegaard described is not enough to serve as the starting point for our faith. Trust involves commitment and risk, yes, but we trust in those we have somehow come to know. It is because of what we learn about God's identity through the biblical narratives that we trust in this God. It is only because some of the content of those narratives underlies our faith that we can be sure that it is this

God, and not some idol of our own imagining, in whom we trust.[26]

Third, regarding those who take the Bible as authority because it narrates God's identity, they too need to remember that they cannot avoid propositional truth claims altogether. An anecdotal account of who God is need not be historical in detail, but there are crucial points—crucifixion and resurrection, to take obvious cases—where it would seem that Christian faith needs to make particular claims about what happened.[27] In an age dominated as ours is by the thought patterns of science, a turn to literary categories seems to many somehow a way of avoiding the issues, a way of not quite facing up to the question of what's really true.[28] So theologians pursuing this model need to face the truth question honestly.

Moreover, the application of the tools of literary analysis to scripture and the language of narration and identity risk losing, if only in terms of rhetorical force, the sense of the Bible's transforming power. Theologians interested in narrative structure and literary form need to find ways to make their ideas seem vivid and important to ordinary people in the church. The claims "This proposition is true" and "Hear this word and let it transform your life" convey a more dramatic sense of authority than contemporary theologians have yet managed to capture for the claim to witness to the identity of God through narrative.[29] I do not think, however, that we ought to make judgments too early. The call to "tell me the stories of Jesus" speaks to something deep within Christian experience, and I do not believe that the power and importance of literary analysis are all that inexplicable to the average Christian. But the analysis must not forget to show how understanding the narrative is not just a matter of academic interest but can transform the lives of ordinary Christians.

"Come now," said the Lord God to the prophet Isaiah, "let us reason together."[30] I think we do have much to learn from each other, but we can learn only if we recognize that no one approach has all the answers and that different approaches can take the authority of scripture seriously, albeit in different ways. From such conversations we may learn styles of biblical interpretation that are, like the love of God, at once intensely serious and wonderfully free. Ordinary people in our churches are hungering for guidance in these matters, and they get it too rarely. From the conservative side, too often the issue is cast in purely defensive terms that fight for the "maximum quantity" of biblical authority and keep getting us bogged down in apparent conflicts between religion and science or faith and history. On the other hand, evangelical pastors at least talk about the issue. They at any rate provide members of their congregations with an account of the questions and some categories for thinking about them. To that extent, at the lay level it is evangelical churches where the congregations are apt to be most intellectually sophisticated in these matters. In most so-called mainline churches, one will gather from occasional sarcastic references to Jerry Falwell and his ilk that we don't believe what those people believe about the Bible. But one rarely hears even the attempt at an account of what we *do* believe.

No doubt many pastors learn early on that these are dangerous waters and decide to leave well enough alone. Of course the issues do start to get complicated. Seminary education has not always provided adequate preparation for discussing them, and they are not always easy to explain to ordinary folk. But let us not sell our people short. In a recent powerful essay, Edward Farley demands,

> Why do bankers, lawyers, farmers, physicians, homemakers, scientists, salespeople, managers of all sorts, people who carry out all kinds of complicated tasks in their work and home, remain at a literalist, elementary-school level in their religious understanding? How is it that high-school-age church members move easily and quickly into the complex world of computers, foreign languages, DNA, and calculus, and cannot even make a beginning in his-

torical-critical interpretation of a single text of scripture?[31]

One need not agree with Farley's position in its entirety, one need not even think that historical-critical methods provide the most important agenda for study, to concede that we have too often given Christian people inadequate intellectual substance. Historical-critical methods provide one useful set of tools. But even when one reads Augustine or Calvin commenting on scripture, one is struck that, though they may be innocent of such modern methods, the way in which they immersed themselves in the world of the Bible gives their interpretation a richness and a freedom that is hard for us to match. We just do not know the Bible well enough. Too often, therefore, confronted with a particular passage, we have either to accept it in a kind of proof-text way or else reject it. We lack sufficient context to have other interpretive options available. We cannot understand the truth claims of scripture in all their complexity, we cannot find the Bible transforming our lives, we cannot understand the identity of the God portrayed in the biblical narratives unless we have grown thoroughly familiar with the Bible. I think the options I have described provide valuable starting points for thinking about the authority of scripture, and I hope that further discussions might recognize that there is not just one way of taking the Bible seriously. But I also hope that further discussions will consider how to increase biblical literacy among ordinary Christian people, for the Bible cannot function as authority both powerfully and authentically for people who have not learned to know it and love it.[32]

18

NOTES

[1]All these examples cited in Robert Wuthnow, *The Restructuring of American Religion* (Princeton: Princeton University Press, 1988), pp. 73f.

[2]*Ibid.*, p. 75.

[3]*Ibid.*, p. 78. Reference to Robert S. Lynd and Helen Merrell Lynd, *Middletown: A Study in Modern American Culture* (New York: Harvest Books, 1929), pp. 332-334.

[4]*Book of Confessions* (PCUSA), 8.18.

[5]Rudolf Bultmann, *New Testament and Mythology and Other Basic Writings*, trans. Schubert M. Ogden (Philadelphia: Fortress Press, 1984), p. 4.

[6]David H. Kelsey, *The Uses of Scripture in Recent Theology* (Philadelphia: Fortress Press, 1975). Kelsey lays out his typology in chapters 2-4. Scripture, he says, can function as authority for theology in terms of its doctrines (Warfield), its concepts (Bartsch), its narrative (Wright), its presentation of the identity of an agent (Barth), its images (Thornton), its symbols (Tillich), or its presentation of a form of self-understanding (Bultmann).

[7]Charles Hodge, *Systematic Theology*, vol. 1 (New York: Charles Scribner's Sons, 1872), p. 10.

[8]*Ibid.*, p. 163.

[9]*Ibid.*, pp. 156f.

[10]*Ibid.*, p. 170. Calvin used many of the same qualifications. For a good summary, see William J. Bouwsma, *John Calvin: A Sixteenth Century Portrait* (Oxford: Oxford University Press, 1988), pp. 118-125.

[11]Clark H. Pinnock, "How I Use the Bible in Doing Theology," in Robert K. Johnston, *The Use of the Bible in Theology: Evangelical Options* (Atlanta: John Knox, 1985), p. 18.

[12]*Ibid.*, pp. 23-24.

[13]Athanasius, *Life of Antony*, trans. H. Ellershaw, *Nicene and Post-Nicene Fathers*, 2nd series, vol. 4 (Grand Rapids: Eerdmans, 1957), p. 196.

[14]*Ibid.*, p. 195.

[15]Augustine, *Confessions*, trans. Rex Warner (New York: Mentor-Omega Books, 1963), pp. 182f.

[16]Albert Schweitzer, *The Quest of the Historical Jesus*, trans. W. Montgomery (New York: Macmillan, 1961), p. 403.

[17]Rudolf Bultmann, "New Testament and Mythology," in Hans Werner Bartsch, *Kerygma and Myth*, trans. Reginald H. Fuller (New York: Harper and Row, 1961), p. 22. At this point, Fuller's translation seems to me a bit better than Ogden's. See also Rudolf Bultmann, "Die Krisis des Glaubens," *Glauben und Verstehen*, vol. 2 (Tubingen: J.C.B. Mohr, 1952), p. 16.

[18]Rudolf Bultmann, "Bultmann Replies to His Critics," *Kerygma and Myth*, p. 211.

[19]Paul Tillich, *Dynamics of Faith* (New York: Harper and Brothers, 1958), p. 34.

[20]Soren Kierkegaard, *Philosophical Fragments*, trans. David Swenson (Princeton: Princeton University Press, 1962), p. 130.

[21]James H. Cone, *God of the Oppressed* (New York: Seabury Press, 1975),

pp. 111f. Even in this passage, and more clearly elsewhere, Cone also draws in part on my third model of scriptural authority, the Bible as the narrative of God's identity. He owes that theme both to the African-American tradition and to his own scholarly work on Karl Barth. But I think this passage does illustrate my second model at work.

[22]George A. Lindbeck, *The Nature of Doctrine* (Philadelphia: Westminster Press, 1984), especially chapter 6.

[23]In the "Royal Man" sections of the *Church Dogmatics*, David Kelsey writes, Karl Barth treats "scripture as a source of anecdotes about what Jesus said or did which one would tell to show 'what he was like.'" Kelsey, *The Uses of Scripture in Recent Theology*, p. 43.

[24]See especially Hans W. Frei, *The Identity of Jesus Christ* (Philadelphia: Fortress Press, 1975).

[25]Charles M. Wood, "Hermeneutics and the Authority of Scripture," in Garrett Green, ed., *Scriptural Authority and Narrative Interpretation* (Philadelphia: Fortress Press, 1987), p.13.

[26]These were points early made against Bultmann, even by his own students. See for instance Ernst Kasemann, *New Testament Questions of Today*, trans. W. J. Montague (Philadelphia: Fortress Press, 1969), p. 52; Heinz Zahrnt, *The Historical Jesus*, trans. J. S. Bowden (New York: Harper and Row, 1963), p. 93; Gerhard Ebeling, *Theology and Proclamation*, trans. John Riches (London: Collins, 1966), p. 68.

[27]I have discussed this point at greater length in "Paul Ricoeur and Postliberal Theology: A Conflict of Interpretations?" *Modern Theology* 4 (October 1987), pp. 46-48, and in chapter 10 of *Unapologetic Theology* (Louisville: Westminster/John Knox Press, 1989). Hans Frei acknowledged that there are points where the narrative "allows and even forces us to ask the question, 'Did this actually take place?'" Frei, *The Identity of Jesus Christ*, p. 140.

[28]This seems to be the argument of John Barton in *People of the Book? The Authority of the Bible in Christianity* (Louisville: Westminster/John Knox Press, 1988).

[29]Jeffrey Stout, who is quite sympathetic to this style of theology, worries that it can never "win a wide hearing." Jeffrey Stout, *Ethics After Babel* (Boston: Beacon Press, 1988), p. 186.

[30] Isaiah 1:18 (RSV).

[31]Edward Farley, *The Fragility of Knowledge* (Philadelphia: Fortress Press, 1988), p. 92.

[32] An essay of mine that somewhat overlaps with this one is found in *To Confess the Faith Today*, ed. Jack Stotts and Jane Dempsey Douglass (Philadelphia: Westminster/John Knox Press, 1990).

2

The Nature of Biblical Authority: A Conservative Perspective

Jack W. Cottrell

A *conservative* by definition is one who is inclined to conserve or preserve the historical, traditional state of things. Thus the conservative view of the Bible is the orthodox or traditional view, as contrasted with newer views. (This does not imply an uncritical, unquestioning acceptance of tradition, nor a refusal to consider newer views.) To be more specific, the basic essence of conservatism *is* its particular view of biblical authority, namely, the view that is considered to have been the consensus of Christendom from its beginning until modern times. It is the view that defines biblical authority in terms of the truthfulness of the contents of scripture and that understands its contents to be revealed and/or inspired by God in such a way that it is basically without error.[1]

In the larger spectrum of contemporary theological views, such a conservatism would include practically all who call themselves "fundamentalists,"[2] and most who would be comfortable with the designation "conservative evangelical."

Within the spectrum of conservatism itself, there are extremes from which most would carefully distance themselves. This includes the radical fringe that attaches inspiration and inerrancy to such things as the 1611 King James Version or to the Hebrew vowel points. It also includes those who call themselves conservatives but who hold to a view of inspiration that does not entail at least the *concept* of inerrancy (regardless of their feeling about the word itself).

The other term to be defined is *authority*. In its most comprehensive sense, authority is the right to establish norms for belief and conduct, the right to command others to conform to these norms, and the rightful power to enforce conformity by punishing wrongdoers. Some would add that it is the right "to act...without consulting anyone or anything else."[3] Some would argue, as does Bernard Ramm, that "in a very real sense all authority is at root *personal*."[4] That is, authority is an attribute that applies only to persons. Christians would certainly affirm that all authority, in the above comprehensive sense, ultimately belongs to a personal being, namely, God.

Is it proper, then, to say that authority can be an attribute of a written document such as the Bible? Yes, but only in connection with the very first aspect of authority as defined above. A document as such cannot possess the right to *command* and to *enforce* and to *act*; these are things that only persons can do. But the authority of a document can properly be described as "the right to establish norms for belief and conduct" because this aspect of authority is inherent in *truth as such*, whether considered in connection with a person or in the abstract (as in a document).[5] R.P.C. Hanson distinguishes between *external* authority as "that attaching to a person," and *internal* authority as "the authority residing in convincing argument or weighty moral or spiritual example or experience."[6] Biblical authority is of the latter or internal type.

Concisely stated, the authority of the Bible is its right to compel belief and action (i.e., to establish norms for belief and conduct).[7] The word *compel* is used in a moral sense only; it does not involve any kind of physical compulsion. Here it means "to persuade" or "to place under an obligation." The *right* to compel belief and action is not the same as the power to do so.[8] When the Bible compels belief and action, it does so by right. We affirm the Bible's authority in this proper sense when we say that it alone is our rule of faith and practice.

Our goal in the rest of this paper is to explain why conservatives believe the Bible has such authority, why it has the right to compel belief and action.

The Bible's Authority Lies in Its Truth

In simplest terms, the Bible is authoritative because it is true. The most vital or crucial aspect of its authority is a function of its truthfulness. To the extent that it is true, it has the right to compel belief and action. To the extent that its truthfulness cannot be asserted, the Bible has no authority. Carl Henry says, "What guarantees the authority of scripture is their [sic] divine truth."[9]

Truth here is understood in the sense of correspondence with reality. A statement is true to the extent that it corresponds with the way things really are.[10] Some object to this concept of truth because perceptual or observational difficulties make it impossible to determine "the way things really are." This may be so in an absolute sense, but this is more of a technicality than a practical problem. In any case, the correspondence concept of truth is the only one that deserves to be called "truth"; this alone is truth in the literal sense of the word. To define truth in any other way is to define it metaphorically. Strictly speaking, truth is a property only of *propositions* (i.e., statements, affirmations, indicative sentences). These are called cognitive statements or truth-claims; they can be either true or false. Non-cognitive utterances include such things as commandments and questions and are not properly described as either true or false.

When we speak of the truthfulness of the Bible, then, we are speaking only of those parts or those statements that are actually claiming to be true (i.e., to correspond to reality). A considerable portion of the Bible is non-cognitive, and some parts, though cognitive in form, are intentionally figurative or parabolic in essence. The concept of truthfulness does not apply to these parts (which are nonetheless authoritative in the direct sense discussed below on pp. 31ff.). For our purposes here, though, we shall include the category of commandments within the scope of truth. This may be justified by the fact that the Bible's commands correspond to the moral reality of both God and man and thus are true in the sense of corresponding to reality. Thus they bear the authority of truth and have the right to compel action.[11]

The relation between truth and authority as set forth here applies to all truth, whether found in the Bible or anywhere else. It is a general principle that truth has the right to compel belief and action. *Any* true statement has this right, no matter who says it. Once a statement has been determined to be true, we are under a moral obligation to believe it (or to obey it, if it is a "true" commandment).

According to the conservative view, biblical authority is simply a particular instance of this general principle. The authority of scripture is a function of its truthfulness. Why should any specific biblical statement be believed (or obeyed)? Simply because it is true. Any part of the Bible that professes to be true but is not actually has no authority; it cannot rightfully compel belief or action.[12]

Herein lies the basic weakness of non-conservative views, which generally see the Bible as having the right—or at least the ability—to compel belief and action, apart from the question of whether it is true or not. Such a view of authority may be called the functional or experiential view, because it says that the Bible's authority is its ability to function in a particular way (whether by intention or not).[13] Usually it functions to produce a certain kind of experience in the heart and life of its readers. To the conservative mind this is not true authority. A message may compel with *more* than its truth, which scripture does; but any message that compels *without regard* to its truth or untruth lacks authority, i.e., it has no *right* to compel belief and action. One cannot validly accept a statement as authoritative unless he or she knows or at least believes it is true.

The Bible Is True Because It Is the Word of God

Even if we accept the fact that truth is inherently authoritative, this still leaves us with a crucial question, namely, how can we be sure a given statement is true? Basically there are two ways to be sure. We can *know* it by verifying it ourselves (via experience or investigation) or we can *believe* the testimony of someone whom we have reason to trust.

For example, let's say that you have promised your daughter that if she gets all As in her first full year of college, you will buy her a new car. At the end of the year she calls from college and says, "I did it! I got all As for the year!" If you suspect that your daughter's self-interest might lead her to exaggerate, you can examine the grade report with your own eyes or even check with each of her teachers to verify the truth of the statement. But if you trust your daughter, her testimony alone is sufficient to convince you of this particular truth. Either way, being satisfied that it is the truth, you are then compelled to act and thus to keep your promise.

Our approach to the Bible is basically no different from this. Are its statements true? How do we know? One way is to verify them ourselves through our own research and investigation. Was there a king of Assyria named Sargon, as Isaiah 20:1 claims? Was there a king of Babylon named Belshazzar, as Daniel 5:1 claims? If he was king and Daniel was second only to him, how could Daniel be the "third ruler" in the kingdom, as Daniel 5:16, 29 claims? Was Herod really the tetrarch of Galilee in the fifteenth year of the reign of Tiberius Caesar, as Luke 3:1 claims? Was there really a man named Jesus who was crucified under Pontius Pilate, as the Gospels claim? Did he really arise from the dead, as claimed throughout the New Testament?

The truth (or possible falsehood) of biblical claims such as these can in principle be verified by archaeological research and historical analysis. Statements about historical events are statements about situations that leave an objective imprint in their wake. The unqualified success of biblical archaeology in uncovering much of this imprint is a well-known story. Thus the historicity of many details of the biblical narratives has been established. Conservatives as a rule believe that an honest application of the ordinary rules of historical analysis to the biblical records is sufficient to establish the historicity even of the resurrection of Jesus.[14]

The problem with this approach to verifying the truth of the Bible is that it is so limited in its application. For one thing, though it properly applies to statements of a historical nature, only a small fraction of biblical claims about historical events have been (and probably ever will be) individually verified thereby. The fact that the evidence thus far uncovered seems to be unanimous in its support of the Bible's historical details certainly gives us a *prima facie* reason to trust its historical claims in general, but still the bulk of this material is without any direct or specific support whatsoever.

Another limitation of this approach (of investigative verification) is that it applies only to statements about objective, historical events. By its very nature it cannot verify the validity of commands; it cannot verify the truth of statements about the meaning or interpretation of historical events; it cannot verify the truth of statements about the future, such as prophecies and promises; it cannot verify the truth of statements about events in the spiritual realm. The reality to which such statements correspond leaves no historical residue to be discovered by even the most diligent archaeological or historical research. And it is immediately evident that these kinds of statements are the heart and soul of theistic and Christian faith.

This leads us to the other way of being sure that a statement is true, namely, accepting the testimony of someone whom we have reason to trust. Some non-conservatives have in fact approached biblical authority in this way by calling it the "authority of the eyewitness." I.e., because the

Bible is the testimony of those who actually witnessed the crucial events of salvation-history, it has a unique authority based on chronological primacy.[15] Kelsey speaks of "the consensus view that scripture is authoritative because it provides our *normative link* with God's self-disclosure."[16]

Surely there is some validity to this approach. The word of an eyewitness is generally accepted as more trustworthy than second-hand or third-hand testimony. And certainly much of the narrative material in the Bible *is* related to us by eyewitnesses whom we have good reason to trust and thereby bears the authority of truth. But this approach to authority also suffers from severe limitations. With reference to many significant events the biblical records are not represented as being the testimony of eyewitnesses (e.g., the events of Genesis, the virgin birth). But even more serious is the fact that, as noted above, the Bible's most crucial truth-claims are not about historical events as such and thus are not observable by eyewitnesses.

Where does this leave us, then, with regard to the truth and thus the authority of statements that contain the very essence of Christianity? How can we be sure that "in the beginning God created the heavens and the earth"? How can we be sure that Jesus of Nazareth is truly "the Christ, the Son of the living God"? We may know from eyewitness accounts that Jesus died on a cross, but how can we be sure that "He Himself is the propitiation for our sins; and not for ours only, but also for those of the whole world"? How can we know that remission of sins is truly given in Christian baptism? How can we know that making a "graven image" of God is wrong?

These are not the kinds of things that can be established by historical investigation or by the testimony of eyewitnesses. Why, then, do we accept them as true? Because these and other such biblical statements are the testimony or word of someone we have reason to trust, namely, GOD HIMSELF. Here is the heart of the conservative view of biblical authority: The Bible is entirely true and thus authoritative because it is the Word—indeed, the very *words*—of God.

28

God is the ultimate authority in all aspects of the term. He has authority inherently just because of who He is: the transcendent, infinite, omnipotent, omniscient Creator. This inherent authoritativeness applies to His words. Any words spoken by God are *ipso facto* true, and therefore authoritative. They compel belief and action just because they are the words of God. Unlike the words of those whose authority is only delegated and thus derived, the authority of God's words is not relative; it is absolute.

This is why conservatives believe it is crucial to understand that the Bible is the Word (or words) of God: This is the ONLY WAY its truthfulness, and thus its authority, can be guaranteed in reference to those parts of its contents that are most crucial for our Christian faith. Here is the point of the traditional doctrines of revelation, inspiration, and inerrancy. Revelation and inspiration are the *reason why* the Bible can be called the Word of God, and inerrancy is the *result* of its being the Word of God.

To reveal is to disclose, to uncover, to unveil, to make known that which was previously unknown. God is the subject of revealing action in many different ways, including the disclosure of truth to and through His apostles and prophets. *Revelation* is both the act of revealing and the product of that act. The latter includes the body of divinely given truth communicated to us in the form of words. Large portions of the Bible are revelation in this sense, i.e., they are words formulated in the very mind of God and disclosed to us through His spokesmen.

Revelation thus includes the direct and indirect communication of truth from God to others. *Inspiration* is involved in *indirect* communication, i.e., when God uses a spokesman or prophet to mediate this revelation (or other truth) to third parties. Revelation can be given without inspiration; the latter becomes involved only when God uses spokesmen to pass His revelation along to others. Inspiration is His divine control of the spokesman's mind and mouth for the purpose of guaranteeing the accurate transmission of His revealed truth. Also, inspiration can be given without revelation; not every inspired statement is a revealed statement. God sometimes desires a person to accurately transmit certain facts and truths known to him by means other than revelation; thus God exerts His divine control just to guarantee the accuracy of that transmission. Thus we may define inspiration as the supernatural influence exerted by the Holy Spirit upon prophets and apostles, which enabled them to communicate without error or omission those truths, received through revelation or otherwise, that God has deemed necessary for our salvation and service.

In light of this distinction and this relation between revelation and inspiration, we can rightly say that although not all of the Bible is revealed, it is all inspired. Both revelation and inspiration together or either by itself is sufficient to produce a message that is rightly called *the Word of God*. The revealed and inspired portions of the Bible are certainly the Word of God, but so are those parts that are not revealed but only inspired. Though the latter comes from human experiences and reflections, they are so guarded by the Holy Spirit in their transmission that they have God's full approval and guarantee of accuracy.[17]

This is the sense in which the quality of *inerrancy* is ascribed to the Bible. Because it is God's revealed and inspired word, it *must* be inerrant, because an all-knowing and upright God could not and would not allow any errors, either deliberate or unintentional, to remain in the work to which He has given His stamp of approval. Thus "God's Word" is by definition "God's inerrant Word."[18]

Descriptions of this view of biblical authority are often plagued by unfortunate extremes on the part of its proponents and unfair caricatures by its opponents. Most conservatives vehemently repudiate both. For example, virtually no conservatives hold to a dictation or mediumistic theory of inspiration, despite the persistent attempts of some non-conservatives to link such a view with inerrancy.[19] *Verbal* inspiration means that even the words of the Bible are inspired, and not just its thoughts; it does not entail the idea that they were inspired by some form of dictation.

Related to this is the accusation that the conservative view leaves no room for a human side to the Bible. Such a criticism is quite untrue, being based on the unwarranted notion that humanness *requires* the presence of errors. This is no more true than the idea that the humanity of Jesus would require Him to commit sin.

Another extreme is the idea that inspiration and/or inerrancy somehow applies to certain copies or translations of the Bible. Though some fanatical fundamentalists do claim that the King James Version is revealed, inspired, and inerrant, no responsible conservative would hold to such a view. These qualities apply only to the original text as produced by the original writers of scripture.[20]

To speak of the Bible as the Word (or words) of God does entail a commitment to the possibility and reality of *word revelation*.[21] Most non-conservatives object to word revelation on philosophical grounds.[22] They say, for example, that it is metaphysically impossible for the transcendent, infinite God to speak understandably to finite beings; "the finite cannot contain the infinite." Conservatives reply that what some see as the problem is actually the solution. Rather than being a barrier to verbal communication, God's transcendence is the very thing that makes it possible. Just because He is infinitely powerful and wise, he is able to bridge the Creator-creature gap with understandable speech. The fact that we are created in God's image prepares us to be on the receiving end of this speech.

A related objection is that any alleged word revelation would have to be deposited among human beings in particular historical and cultural contexts and thus would be limited by the relativities of such contexts. Since "the relative cannot contain the absolute," any such alleged revelations could not be absolute truth with absolute authority. Conservatives reply in two ways. First, this objection confuses truth with the *understanding* of truth. It is true that the contents of any statement are relative to the historical context in which it is spoken. But this affects not the truth and authority of the statement but only cross-cultural attempts to understand it.

Thus historical relativity is a factor in biblical interpretation, not biblical authority.[23] This makes critical Bible study all the more essential, not to determine whether a particular biblical statement is true, but to determine what it means.[24] Second, this objection exaggerates the problem of cultural relativity, implying that it is all but impossible to have reliable communication across cultural boundaries. While such is sometimes difficult, it is seldom impossible. We do it all the time, and usually quite successfully. The phenomenon of translation from one language to another is an example of it, while the translation of the Bible itself into countless languages is an example of its success.[25]

The conservative concludes that there is no valid objection to word revelation as such, or to the Bible's being called "the Word(s) of God" on such grounds. But there is also a more direct connection: (a) the Bible is the Word of God, (b) therefore the Bible is authoritative *just because* it is the word of God and by that fact alone, since *every* word that God speaks bears inherent authority.[26]

This latter point leads us to the bottom-line conclusion for conservatives: There is no qualitative difference between the authority of scripture and the authority of God. This does not mean that the two concepts are identical.[27] For instance, there is a significant quantitative difference between them, in that the authority of the Bible does not exhaust the totality of God's authority; the latter is much broader in scope than biblical authority alone. Qualitatively, however, there is no difference. This is true because there is no difference between the authority of a *person* and the authority of the *words* he speaks, whoever that person is.[28] It may be true that authority is personal, but there is nothing more personal than the words that come from the heart and mind of a person. Jesus shows this inseparability in His rebuke, "And why do you call Me, 'Lord, Lord,' and do not do what I say?" (Luke 6:46).[29]

The only way to deny that the authority of scripture is the authority of God is to deny that scripture is the Word of God in any real sense. This of course is what non-conservatives do. For example, in this Barthian or post-Barthian era many will affirm that Jesus alone is the *true* Word of God, while the Bible is the "word of God" only in some distant or figurative sense. This permits them to distinguish between the authority of the Bible and the authority of God (or Christ), the latter alone being called absolute.[30] The old platitude, "Our authority is a person, not a book," is heralded widely.[31] But this is a false choice, because the Book in question is the revealed/ inspired Word of the Person in question. Carl Henry rightly says, "A divinely given word mediated by the Logos of God through prophets and apostles is just as authoritative as that spoken directly by the incarnate Logos himself."[32]

This leaves one final question to be discussed, namely, how do we know the Bible is the Word of God? Critics accuse conservatives of circular reasoning at this point, declaring that their view of the Bible is established by deductive rather than by the preferred inductive process. The alleged circularity is said to take the form of beginning with (i.e., presupposing the truth of) the Bible's *general* statements about itself (e.g., John 10:35; 2 Tim. 3:16) and deducing therefrom the inspiration and inerrancy of each *particular* passage of scripture. For example, "All scripture is God-breathed; Genesis 1:1 is scripture; therefore Genesis 1:1 is God-breathed." Or, "Scripture cannot be broken; Matthew 1:1 is scripture; therefore Matthew 1:1 cannot be broken." The crucial part of the criticism is that the conservative assumes the truth of the general premise uncritically and thus bases his whole case on an unproven assumption.

Is this a fair representation of conservatism? For the most part, it is not. We grant that many conservatives may think this way, being moved more by inherited piety than by reason. We recognize also that one major branch of scholarly conservative apologetics consciously adopts an approach similar to this. It is called *presuppositionalism* and is limited mainly to certain Calvinists who follow the likes of Cornelius Van Til and Gordon H. Clark. But we must insist that this is *not* the traditional or mainstream conservative approach to biblical authority.[34] There is no circular reasoning; there is no captivity to deductivism.

It is true that the first step in the process is to examine the Bible to see what claims the biblical writers make for the whole body of writings known as scripture.[35] This is one of the main points in the many detailed studies of what the Bible says about revelation, inspiration, and inerrancy. Emphasis falls on such general statements as "Scripture cannot be broken" (John 10:35); "All Scripture is inspired by God [God-breathed]" (2 Tim. 3:16); and "No prophecy of Scripture is a matter of one's own interpretation, for no prophecy was ever made by an act of human will, but men moved by the Holy Spirit spoke from God" (2 Peter 1:20-21). Also emphasized is Paul's general characterization of the Old Testament as "the oracles [the very words] of God" (Rom. 3:2).

But this is not the end of the matter; it is only the first step. Even if it can be established exegetically that such passages as the above do indeed claim that scripture as a whole is the inspired and inerrant Word of God, conservatives do *not* blindly assume that this is true just because "the Bible tells us so." Rather, the next step is to ask the question, "Are there any good reasons for believing that such claims are true?" Here is where *induction* enters, as these claims are examined inductively in the study of Christian evidences. This discipline looks for both internal and external evidence to support the Bible's claims to be of divine origin. It considers such things as the unity of the Bible, its fulfilled prophecies, its remarkable accuracy as determined by archaeology and historical investigation, and its internal consistency. Such facts and phenomena, cumulatively (i.e., inductively) considered, are taken by conservatives to be more than adequate grounds for accepting the Bible's general claims about itself. *Only* when such reasons have been given for accepting these general claims do we then go on to deduce from them the truth of the other individual parts of scripture.

The full statement of the conservative case for biblical authority is as follows: I. The Bible is authoritative in the sense that it has the right to compel belief and action. II. The Bible has this right because it is true, in the sense that its claims correspond to reality. III. The Bible is true and can be confidently accepted as such because it is the Word—even the very *words*—of God. IV. That the Bible is the Word of God is accepted as true because it is established by inductive reasoning in the form of Christian evidences.

We should note carefully that this does not elevate reason to a role of authority higher than that of the Bible itself. So to affirm "would be to use the word 'authority' in a quite different sense," says Hanson. *"Reason* is the means whereby we reach religious convictions, not the matter which affords the material for making our judgments."[36] That is, it is merely the means by which we determine what *is* authoritative and what is not. Ramm is more specific:

> Reason has been made a religious authority by some writers on the subject, but reason is a *mode* of apprehension. If reason apprehends the truth, it is the truth apprehended which is authoritative, not reason. A man's reason apprehends the authority of the state, or distinguishes a true from a false claim to authority. Reason lays bare the grounds for authority. But the object of reason is the truth, and authority rests in what is apprehended, not in the instrument of apprehension.[37]

In other words, we approach the Bible's claims to truth and authority just as we would approach similar claims from any other document or person. If someone claims to have authority over us, we ask for the evidence; e.g., "Show me your badge." The acceptance of authority on any level is a rational decision based on evidence. Thus, though he does not mean it in this same sense, Barr is correct to say that conservatism (or fundamentalism) "is actually a rationalist position."[38] This should not raise any eyebrows. As Henry says, "Evangelicals need not tremble and take to the hills whenever others charge us with rationalism, since not every meaning of that term is objectionable."[39]

Thus we do not accept the authority of the Bible blindly, but use our reason to identify and verify it as the Word of God and thus the very embodiment of divine authority in our midst. But once it has been so identified and verified, we are compelled to submit totally to it, even with our minds.

Conclusion

In the final analysis there are only two choices in our quest for a final authority: divine truth and human experience. Conservatives accept the Bible's authority because they see it as divine truth. That is, its authority is determined by its origin or source or *cause*. When non-conservatives reject the nature of the Bible as divine truth but still attempt to retain some concept of biblical authority; the only alternative is to locate that authority in the Bible's *effect*, i.e., in its ability to produce some kind of experience in, or have a certain kind of impact upon, those who read it or hear its message proclaimed.[40]

The problem with the latter approach is that it leaves us with no standard by which we can determine what is a valid experience and what is a misleading and destructive experience, and by which we can defend the Bible's ultimate authority over against the claims of its rivals. Depending on how it is understood, the Bible itself can produce a multiplicity of experiences; and many of these cannot be differentiated from the experiences produced by other religious books and leaders and even secular leaders at times. The Christian has no more reason to accept his experience as valid, along with the whole theological system built upon it, than does the Mormon, the Muslim, the Jehovah's Witness, the Buddhist, or the Occultist. We are left with religious relativism, where the natural conclusion is that "Jesus is not the only Savior," i.e., the only one whose Word can produce a valid experience.

To the conservative mind, unless the Bible is *true*, it has no authority, no right to compel belief and action, and no ability to produce *valid* religious experience. Only a Bible that is objectively true prior to our experience of it can claim any authority over us and at the same time produce within us experiences that will prove to be eternally valid.

36

NOTES

(Scripture quotations are from the New American Standard Version.)

[1] Whether inerrancy has actually been Christendom's view from the beginning or whether it is a view articulated only in the later centuries of church history, is a question that will not materially affect our discussion here. Jack Rogers and Donald McKim support the latter view in *The Authority and Interpretation of the Bible* (San Francisco: Harper and Row, 1979), while John D. Woodbridge argues for the former view in *Biblical Authority: A Critique of the Rogers/McKim Proposal* (Grand Rapids: Zondervan, 1982).

[2] James Barr tends to use the terms *fundamentalist* and *conservative* interchangeably and says that fundamentalism involves the idea that "the doctrinal and practical authority of scripture is necessarily tied to its infallibility and in particular its historical inerrancy" ("The Problem of Fundamentalism Today," in his book *The Scope and Authority of the Bible* [Philadelphia: Westminster Press, 1980], p. 65). While acknowledging that many who hold this view prefer not to be called "fundamentalists" but rather "evangelicals" or "conservative evangelicals," Barr considers the latter terms inappropriate for those who hold this view of biblical authority and thus labels them all "fundamentalists" (*Fundamentalism* [Philadelphia: Westminster Press, 1977], pp. 2-5). We cannot accept this approach, however. Though their view of biblical authority may be the same, fundamentalists and conservative evangelicals differ significantly enough on other points to warrant the different designations.

[3] William Barclay, *By What Authority?* (Valley Forge: Judson Press, 1974), p. 7. See also H.D. McDonald, "Bible, Authority of," *Evangelical Dictionary of Theology*, ed. Walter A. Elwell (Grand Rapids: Baker, 1984). He says, "In its personal reference authority is the right and capacity of an individual to perform what he wills" (p. 138). Such a right, of course, is inherent in God alone, though He may delegate such authority in restricted spheres to human beings (e.g., civil government, parents, church elders). Carl Henry says, "God alone is the absolute power of decision" (*God, Revelation and Authority, Vol. IV, God Who Speaks and Shows: Fifteen Theses, Part Three* [Waco: Word Books, 1979], p. 25). [Hereafter, Henry's work will be abbreviated as *GRA*.]

[4] Bernard Ramm, *The Pattern of Religious Authority* (Grand Rapids: Eerdmans, 1957), p. 14.

[5] Ramm distinguishes the category of *veracious authority*, or "the authority of veracity of truth" (*ibid.*, p. 12). He recognizes that this would appear to be an impersonal kind of authority, but says that even this derives ultimately from the person of God (p. 14). Sometimes the connection is only indirect, though: "Veracious authority is directly or indirectly the authority of a person" (pp. 25f.).

[6] R.P.C. Hanson, "Authority," *The Westminster Dictionary of Christian Theology*, ed. Alan Richardson & John Bowden (Philadelphia: Westminster Press, 1983), p. 58.

[7] Millard Erickson says it is "the right of the Bible to prescribe the belief and actions of Christians" (*Concise Dictionary of Christian Theology* [Grand

Rapids: Baker Book House, 1986], p. 21). Carl Henry says, "When dealing with authority we are concerned with necessity or compulsion, with what must be believed or must be done" (GRA, IV:75).

[8] Not everything that actually compels belief and action has the right to do so. Bullies may compel action by threat of physical harm; charlatans and demagogues may compel belief through charm or charisma alone. Even a document filled with mistakes and lies can compel belief and action if it is cleverly and persuasively written.

[9] GRA, IV:75. This statement would be true even without the word divine.

[10] Strictly speaking the correspondence is not between the words of a statement and the reality it represents, as if certain words inherently correspond to particular aspects of reality. All words are "conventional signs," as Carl Henry says (GRA, IV:106). The crucial correspondence is between the reality as such and our concept of it. A statement is true to the extent that it either represents or provokes a concept that corresponds to reality, in accordance with the meaning assigned to words by convention.

[11] Carl Henry notes, "Imperatives are not as such true or false propositions; but they can be translated into propositions...from which cognitive inferences can be drawn." For example, "Thou shalt not kill" means "To kill is wrong" (GRA, III:417, 477).

[12] The Bible's truth (and therefore authority) is not its only appeal to humankind. Especially, the truth of the Gospel has a non-cognitive appeal as well; it draws us emotionally and aesthetically and existentially as well as intellectually. In popular terms, it appeals to the heart as well as to the head. But a "gospel" that is not true (see Gal. 1:6-9), though it may be presented in a way that appeals to the heart, has no true authority. It is a pseudo-gospel.

[13] Carl Henry observes, "The current tendency is to redefine biblical authority functionally....The Bible is said to be authoritative merely in the manner in which it operates existentially in the life of the believing community" (GRA, IV:68). Henry gives numerous examples, citing often James Barr (e.g., his Fundamentalism) and David H. Kelsey's The Uses of Scripture in Recent Theology (Philadelphia: Fortress Press, 1975), which is itself a survey of non-conservative views. Cf. Henry, GRA, vol. IV, chs. 3 & 4.

[14] See, for example, John W. Montgomery's History and Christianity (Downers Grove: InterVarsity Press, 1965).

[15] R.P.C. Hanson says that when "judged by modern conceptions of authority...the Bible will be considered as the unique witness to the acts of God in history by which he makes himself known to all men and demands their response" ("Authority," p. 59). W.B. Blakemore has said, "The authority of the New Testament lies in its primacy and uniqueness, not in infallibility" ("The Place of Theology in the Life of the Church," The Scroll 47 [Summer 1955], p. 22).

[16] Kelsey, The Uses of Scripture in Recent Theology, p. 47. Italics added.

[17] Carl Henry comments thus on the relation between inspiration and

38

authority: "The Christian apostles affirmed not only the divine authority of scripture but also its supernatural inspiration. Any repudiation of divine inspiration as a property of the biblical text they would have considered an attack on the authority of scripture. In their view scripture is authoritative, because divinely inspired, and as such, is divine truth" (*GRA*, IV:68).

[18] Not all conservatives are comfortable with the term *inerrancy*, usually as the result of a misunderstanding of what is intended by the word. Thus a refusal to use the word *inerrancy* does not necessarily exclude one from the ranks of conservatism. The International Council on Biblical Inerrancy has attempted to clarify what is usually meant by the term. See "The Chicago Statement on Biblical Inerrancy," an appendix to *Inerrancy*, ed. Norman Geisler (Grand Rapids: Zondervan, 1979), pp. 493ff. (see especially p. 496). See also Jack Cottrell, "Dedicated to Scriptural Inerrancy: the Biblical/Theological Implications," *The Seminary Review* 30 (September 1984), pp. 95-99.

[19] An example of this kind of false representation comes from Charles F. Lamb, who says conservatives insist that "each word in the Bible...is dictated by God" ("The Only Creed," *The Disciple* [October 1984], p. 11).

[20] The original *text* is different from the original *manuscripts*. The faulty idea that inerrancy is irrelevant because it applies only to no-longer-existent "originals" confuses the two. It is true that the original *manuscripts* no longer exist, but with few exceptions the original *text* DOES exist, thanks to the science of textual criticism. Inerrancy is an attribute of the *text*, whether that text appears on the original manuscripts, in a present-day critical edition of the Greek text, or in a faithful translation of the same. For a discussion of this point see Greg Bahnsen, "The Inerrancy of the Autographa," *Inerrancy*, ed. Norman Geisler, pp. 151-193.

[21] See Henry, *GRA*, vol. III, chapters 24-27.

[22] For an exposition of the non-conservative view see John Baillie's classic work, *The Idea of Revelation in Recent Thought* (New York: Columbia University Press, 1956). For a conservative evaluation of it see Ronald Nash, *The Word of God and the Mind of Man* (Grand Rapids: Zondervan, 1982).

[23] This is not to say that these two things can be absolutely separated. Myron Taylor has rightly said that "the authority of the Bible is exercised effectively only through biblical interpretation," and that "we are compelled to interpret that Bible if we expect to encounter its authority," for "the Bible's authority is in its meaning" (*The Lamp* 13 [May 1988], p. 1). That is to say, the authority of the Bible lies not just in its truth as abstractly and formally considered, but also in the *meaning* of that truth as intended by its author. Conservatives believe that in most cases this intended meaning can be discerned with reasonable certainty. (Cf. the Reformation concept of the *clarity* of scripture.)

[24] As Henry says, "In actuality there need be no objection to historical criticism or to form criticism per se....They do not by any inherent necessity either erode or destroy it....What accounts for the adolescent fantasies of biblical criticism are not its legitimate pursuits but its paramour relation-

ships with questionable philosophical consorts" (GRA, IV:81). Thus we reject allegations (such as Barr's) that the conservative view "involves the repudiation of the results of modern critical modes of reading the Bible" (James Barr, *The Scope and Authority of the Bible,* p. 66).

[25] See Henry's discussion of this idea of "the radical relativity of all beliefs and values" in GRA, IV:53-67; 113ff. He declares that "culture may surely shape the beliefs of any given period, but it cannot decide the truth or falsity of those beliefs." He reminds the proponents of cultural relativism that they expect their own statements to be understood cross-culturally; thus they are inconsistent. "Whoever contends that revelation cannot be the carrier of objective truth transcending our social location in history claims a privileged standpoint of personal exemption from that dictum. Nothing in either history or culture precludes transcultural truth. If the relativist can presume to communicate truth that spans cultural boundaries when he affirms historical or cultural relativity, surely the absolutist can do so; moreover, he alone has adequate reason to do so if in fact God has intelligibly disclosed his transcendent will. The truth of God can be stated in all cultures; it does not need to be *re*stated in any culture except by way of linguistic translation and repetition" (p. 53).

[26] Bernard Ramm has said, "The Bible is authoritative because it is the *Word of God* (that is, it is part of the organism of revelation) and for no other reason" (*The Pattern of Religious Authority,* p. 38).

[27] Carl Henry says, "There is, to be sure, a sense in which we ought and must speak exclusively of God as the absolute authority, and acknowledge scriptural authority to be merely derivative and contingent" (GRA, IV:42).

[28] See Jack Cottrell, *The Authority of the Bible* (Grand Rapids: Baker Book House, 1979 reprint), pp. 91f.

[29] Robert Lowery has made this fine statement: "Accepting the lordship of Christ and the authoritativeness of scripture go hand-in-hand. In every single area of our lives, Jesus, the living Word, is to be Lord. Correspondingly, is it not true that the Bible, the written Word, is to be the authoritative guide for what we believe and how we behave as Christians? Unless God has given us a Word that is trustworthy, we will have no court of appeal for deciding what is truly Christian and what is not. To deny scripture's authoritativeness is to deny ultimately Christ's authority." ("Acknowledging the Authoritativeness of Scripture," Part One, *Christian Standard* [Sept. 2, 1984], p. 7.)

[30] Fred Norris says, "The New Testament which we accept as our norm does not ask us to accept it as our final authority. It speaks of Jesus the Christ. It proclaims Him as *the* authority." ("Jesus Is Lord," *Envoy* [January 1977], p. 1.)

[31] See, e.g., William J. Moore, "The Biblical Doctrine of Ministry," *Encounter* 17 (Autumn 1956), p. 387. See also Leroy Garrett, "The Nature of Biblical Authority and the Restoration Movement," printed version of a speech at the North American Christian Convention (Anaheim, CA: July 24, 1974), p. 1: "Authority is not in a book but in a person."

[32] GRA, IV:37. See the full discussion, pp. 35-40, 50-52.

40

[33] James Barr has voiced this criticism: "To a very large extent, the doctrinal statements of modern conservatives base their position about the Bible on one single point: The Bible is authoritative, inspired and inerrant because the Bible itself says so. Because the Bible itself says so, we have to believe it, and if we do not, then nothing in the Bible would have any value." (*Fundamentalism*, p. 260.)

[34] See R.C. Sproul, John Gerstner, and Arthur Lindsley, *Classical Apologetics: A Rational Defense of the Christian Faith and a Critique of Presuppositional Apologetics* (Grand Rapids: Zondervan, 1984).

[35] Critics say that the Bible never makes any claims about itself "in general" or "as a whole," since all the biblical documents were not in existence when most of the specific claims were made. (E.g., see Barr, *Fundamentalism*, p. 78.) This misses the point, however. The biblical claims do not necessarily refer only to certain specific documents in existence at the time, but to a *category* or *class* of writings known as *scripture*. For example, see how naturally 2 Peter 3:15-16, referring to Paul, lumps "all his letters" in the same category as "the rest of the scriptures." For a discussion of this point see Henry, *GRA*, IV:134ff.

[36] R.P.C. Hanson, "Authority," p. 59.

[37] Bernard Ramm, *The Pattern of Religious Authority*, p. 44.

[38] James Barr, *The Scope and Authority of the Bible*, p. 70. He says that "it is perhaps the only really rationalist position widely operative within Christianity today....Nowhere is the rationalism of fundamentalist argument more clear than in the doctrine of the inspiration and infallibility of the Bible itself." (*ibid.*)

[39] *GRA*, III:480. It definitely would be objectionable in the broad sense in which James Draper uses the term, i.e., as anything that constitutes "the human mind as ultimate authority." He includes within this category classical philosophical rationalism, classical empiricism, and mysticism. (James T. Draper, Jr., *Authority: The Critical Issue for Southern Baptists* [Old Tappan, NJ: Revell, 1984], pp. 16f.)

[40] A typical example is James Barr, who says the Bible's authority lies in its ability to *function* in a certain way, in its ability to effect a faith-relation between man and God. It is the "meeting-ground for our encounter with God" (*The Scope and Authority of the Bible*, pp. 53-55). "The authority of the Bible [lies] in the meeting with Christ which it mediated, and not in the acceptance as true of the information or attitudes which it contained" (*ibid.*, pp. 57f.).

A Liberal Response

Barbara S. Blaisdell

In his thoughtful and clear paper, Jack Cottrell argues that the Bible derives its authority from the truthfulness of its contents and that the nature of that authority resides in its ability to persuade us with a compelling argument regarding "norms for belief and conduct." We believe the Bible because it is true and we obey the commands within it because that truth is compelling. On that we can agree. Cottrell goes on to contrast this position with certain non-conservative positions that typically root the Bible's authority in something other than truthfulness (e.g., in its ability "to produce a certain kind of experience in the heart and life of its readers").

There may be those who hold this latter claim. I have heard it argued that the psychological astuteness and the ability of certain biblical passages to provide comfort are evidences of scriptural authority. Others cite the Bible's ability to move us emotionally or they see the depth of beauty in the Bible as literature and argue that it must be inspired and, presumably, therefore authoritative.

I am not one of those non-conservatives. Scriptural ability to move and comfort us is certainly a part of its power and beauty. But it is no substitute for the truth. I, too, want to argue that the Bible derives its authority from the veracity of its claims. And I, too, would argue that the nature of that authority is internal. That is, the Bible must offer convincing arguments for its normative claims. The key difference between my liberal position and the conservative position outlined by Cottrell is not in the valuation of truth or the power of truth but in how we can *know* and recognize the truth.

Cottrell outlines a correspondence epistemology. He argues that *truth* is that which corresponds to reality. He writes, "A statement is true to the extent that it corresponds with the way things really are." He points out that truth defined in this way is limited to those statements known as propositions. In contrast to propositions, questions or commands are non-cognitive utterances that cannot be described as true or false. He goes on to point out, rightly I think, that this definition of truth renders large parts of the Bible outside the realm of truth claims. How can one measure the truth of a parable, for example? It makes no propositional claim to correspondence with facts "out there" in reality. It is an imagined, fictional story. Yet most Christians would want to claim that biblical parables are in some sense true. We will return to this below.

It is at this point that Cottrell moves to exempt the biblical commandments from this linguistic rule. While they are not strict propositions, their veracity can be defended, he argues, because they correspond to the moral reality of both God and humanity. The need for such an exception to the rule points to the weakness of this way of recognizing the truth.

This understanding of truth presupposes that there exists out there a reality apart from our language about that reality, and that the function of language is to match up words with that reality. The difficulty with such an assumption is that it ignores the power of language to order and limit what we experience in reality. Indeed, there are those in the field of physics who argue that not only does our language change reality but our simple observations of events change them.

For example, to say "Jesus wept" is to make a verifiable historical claim. It is logically possible to find witnesses who could corroborate such a claim. But the very language used connotes much more (and much less) about reality than simple correspondence to that reality. We are asked to notice Jesus' weeping as opposed to the weeping of others. One can imagine countless others down through the ages who also have wept upon arriving at a deathbed too late, only to find a loved one already dead. And one can imagine, as described by Luke, the scene where Jesus is weeping over Jerusalem; one can also imagine that thousands and millions of others down through the ages looked across Jerusalem and have wept. And one could verify this as fact: that others have wept and weep over human misery and tragedy. And to mention all those instances would indeed correspond more fully with the facts of reality. Yet Christians do not find it surprising or unusual that we are asked in John and in Luke to notice Jesus' weeping. It is as if that fact means more somehow than the other facts.

For we are asked by the gospel writers to notice an *emotion*, something a purely classical theologian would never "notice" about God. Now John, especially, was clearly influenced by Greek classical theology. But the descriptions of Jesus in Luke and John move beyond that language. The God incarnate who weeps over Jerusalem and weeps at the loss of a beloved friend is not impassible. This is no unmoved mover! One weeps when one's freedom to change the situation is limited. We weep when our children make mistakes, the consequences from which we cannot protect them. We weep for hurricane victims, children who are abused, victims of war and violence, because finally, whatever we do does not undo what is history. In short, we weep at tragedy. The classical Greek mind could not and would not notice God weeping. Yet Luke and John did—and transcended a language in order to do it.

Let me use a less freighted, more mundane, example. I might declare, along with a book belonging to my two-year-old, "There is a cat in the hat." By that statement I already inform my child that mammals are important to notice. (There aren't many toddler books about quarks or other characters from quantum physics. Our language, at this most basic level, has not caught up to science yet.) And the statement, "There is a cat in a hat," corresponds to reality by way of humorous exception. Cats do not, as a rule, wear hats. Yet one might well be able to verify the claim. Or we might prove it false. But whatever facts we verify, Dr. Seuss's parable *The Cat in the Hat*—which is about our attraction to things new and different and exciting and a little bit naughty—somehow rings true. There is indeed something intriguing and marvelous about a cat who shows up on our doorstep on a long rainy day to show us some new games to play. But there is no room to measure its truth or falsehood in Dr. Cottrell's epistemology. There is no way to measure its normative claim—that it is sometimes good to seek something new, exciting, and a little bit naughty.

These weaknesses are understood in part by Cottrell in his explication of the limits of attempting to verify the truth of the Bible. Cottrell claims that we can *know* the truth through verifying it or we can *believe* the testimony of someone we trust. He rightly points out that verification of truth under a correspondence epistemology has severe limitations with regard to the Bible. Much of the Bible is not propositional. Much is parabolic. Such truth claims cannot be measured. One can test the historicity of certain biblical events. You can weigh certain truth claims against reality. But what does one do with a parable or a question? Yet surely we notice that the parable of the good Samaritan makes a normative claim on us. Given these limits in knowing the truth within the bounds of his epistemology, Cottrell argues that we should *believe* the Bible (as opposed to verifying its truth) because it is the testimony of someone we have reason to trust. We should *believe* the Bible because its words are from the very mind of God.

This path is fraught with difficulties too, however. For such a method does not admit full room for moral reflection or coherence or plausibility with our experience. Reason has no authority. It *does not* allow the questions, "Is this teaching moral?" or "Does this make any sense?" Surely two thousand years of church history full of blood and bigotry have shown us that we must ask these questions of *every* claim to truth. Is it moral? Does it make any sense? Is it plausible? I realize that I do a risky thing here—asking such questions of Holy Scripture. But not to ask is to risk far more.

Let me illustrate, as gently and clearly and humbly as I can. In the fifth chapter of the book of Acts, Luke tells a story fraught with problems regarding its claims about God. Luke is describing the church, "the company of those who believe," as being of one heart and soul and as holding all property in common for the good of all. But he illustrates his point by exception. He tells the story of Ananias and his wife Sapphira, Christians who sold their property and gave the proceeds to the apostles for the work of the church. All the proceeds, that is, except some that Ananias held back (with the knowledge of his wife) for themselves for their future—a kind of early ministerial pension plan. Luke tells us that Peter knew what Ananias had done and called him on it in a terse interrogation, closing with the line, "You did not lie to us but to God!" The account goes on: "When Ananias heard these words, he fell down and died" (Acts 5:4-5, NRSV). The next scene in this saga is the entrance of the widow Sapphira. Peter baits her cruelly—asking questions about her finances to which he already knows the answers, catching her in her lie, and closing with a "pastoral" response, "Look, the feet of those who have buried your husband [the first she has heard of his death!] are at the door, and they will carry you out" (Acts 5:9b, NRSV). And Luke tells us that the widow Sapphira fell down and died.

Now Luke, by revelation or inspiration, tells this as if it were historical fact. But what exactly is being claimed about

46

God here? Are we to believe that God has pronounced a death sentence upon this couple for cheating on their tithe, for paying their pledge only after they had paid their other bills? And they found they came up short? Of course, it's dishonorable. How many times have we heard that our commitment to the church should come first. But when we fail in that, does it warrant the death penalty? And if it does warrant such a penalty, then there but by the grace of God go I. And why should God's grace apply to me and not to the Christians Ananias and Sapphira? Is this right? Does this make sense?

I celebrate the fact that I have never heard this passage used as part of a stewardship sermon, in spite of the fact that this is clearly a biblical teaching on the importance of Christian stewardship. The fact that I have not heard it so used tells me that those who have taught me the faith, those who have loved me and nurtured me and taught me about God and to love God, have somehow found this passage inappropriate to the gospel of Jesus Christ. It is not true! And, therefore, it does not have authority,

But if these are indeed words from the very mind of God, then I must tragically, and humbly but forthrightly, say that such a god is not a god I can trust. I am profoundly aware of the difficulties here. The values and morals I espouse, the norms I would invoke to discover or measure the truth of the Bible, are culturally influenced (though they came from people deeply immersed in that Bible). They are, as such, *fallible,* open to corruption by human sin. And I am the foremost among sinners. But if the story of Ananias and Sapphira is true, I must stand with my fellow sinners and be damned with them rather than worship and glorify a capricious god.

This is but one troublesome example. Space permits me only to mention the evil of a reportedly divinely inspired child sacrifice in Genesis 22:9-19 or 2 Kings; or of the bigotry against an entire race of people found on the lips of Jesus in John 8 (referring to all Jews as children of the devil and children of murderers—a reference that would get even a politician kicked out of office. Do we expect so much less of God?). Or we could mention the misogyny of Paul in Ephesians 5 or of the pastorals in 1 Timothy 2, or the support of human slavery in Colossians and Philemon, or the identification of God as the murderer of children in Exodus 12:29 and 13:15. These, too, are biblical teachings. Are they truly to be understood as from the very mind of God?

If, on the other hand, the Bible may be understood as deeply energized by the spirit of God, if it can be understood to be a record of many moments when the human spirit is touched by the divine, then it can also be understood as limited by human perception and tainted by human sin (not necessarily but in accordance with the evidence therein). Then I can comprehend how the Luke who could tell the story about the death of Ananias and the taunting and death of his widow as if it were the will of God. Then I can understand how the very same Luke can make profound and beautiful claims that God is the source of the healing of persons in body, mind, and spirit, a claim that is so important to his writings. With this understanding of the Bible, I can dismiss as tragic Paul's apparent embrace of slavery and the subjugation of women and understand how that same Paul could write:

> There is no longer Jew or Greek, there is no longer slave or free, there is no longer male and female; for all of you are one in Christ Jesus. And if you belong to Christ, then you are Abraham's offspring, heirs according to the promise.
> Galatians 3:28-29, NRSV

If the *best* of the Bible is *of God*, then surely we can heed Paul's admonition:

> Finally, beloved, whatever is true, whatever is honorable, whatever is just, whatever is pure, whatever is pleasing, whatever is commendable, if there is any excellence, and if there is anything worthy of praise, think about these things.
> Philippians 4:8, NRSV

48

And what of the Bible is pure, just, honorable, pleasing, commendable, excellent, and worthy of praise? Christians know it as the gospel of Jesus Christ.

Alice Walker, contemporary American novelist, would summarize that gospel in this way: "God loves all the stuff you love...and a bunch of stuff you don't." God loves all the people we do...and a bunch of people we don't. And God seeks after and demands that God's people seek after what is best, what is beautiful for all of them. Paul summarizes it this way:

> For I am convinced that neither death, nor life, nor angels, nor rulers, nor things present, nor things to come, nor powers, nor height, nor depth, nor anything else in all creation, will be able to separate us from the love of God in Christ Jesus our Lord.
>
> Romans 8:38-39, NRSV

And for that gospel, thanks be to God!

A Moderate Response

Gloria Tate

Dr. Cottrell begins with a definition of the conservative view of biblical authority, a view considered to be the consensus of Christianity from its beginning to modern times. It is important to note that this is an opinion, for some would consider that there never was one single consensus view of biblical authority. On the other hand, the definition given can serve as an accepted point of departure for addressing the subject at hand.

In the following remarks, I wish to focus on the stated conservative position concerning understandings of truth, revelation, and the role of human reason.

The Bible as Truth
Dr. Cottrell begins his explanation of why the Bible has the right to compel belief and action by leading us through a

definition of truth and applying it to the Bible. However, in order to assess the nature of that authority, I believe that one should address the development and origins of the Bible historically rather than merely begin a discussion with the canon as we know it. In order to discern the role of the Bible one must have some idea of the perceptions and intent not only of the original writers but of the Christian community that affirmed the biblical canon.

It is important to note that the Christians who composed the literature of the New Testament in retrospect of the life of Jesus did not attempt to create a stenographic account of Jesus' words and deeds. They exercised great freedom in altering the form of the oral tradition that they possessed. Inasmuch as there seemed to be a preference for oral proclamation in the first and second centuries, it is important to consider that the original intent of producing the document was simply to preserve a valid witness to the existence of Jesus Christ.

I agree that the Bible sets norm for Christians. However, the nature of that norm must also be determined. If we appeal to the wisdom and "inspiration" of early Christians, we should acknowledge that there were several sources of literary material that served as guidance for the life and thought of the early church. The Old Testament, the Apocrypha, the Pseudepigrapha, the words of Jesus, the sayings of the apostles and the living word of the Holy Spirit were all understood as normative in their ability to guide the Christian. Only in the second century did Christians become aware of the need for a singular normative testimony, in response to the controversy created by gnosticism. Thus the formulation of the canon as we now have it occurred over several centuries. This leads us to an understanding of the Bible as a product of historical decisions made by the church, and its existence points to the authority of the church to establish a norm for Christianity.

What then is the authority of scripture in light of this? My response fits the description of Cottrell's non-conservative, for I hold what would be described as a functional or experiential view. scripture serves as a witness and a statement of belief. Whether the Bible corresponds with reality is a valid question when discerning the truth of the Bible. However, one must also ask whether scripture, as recorded, witnesses to a reality or a perception of reality that has validity for us. Paul Tillich states, "Every period of history has a different understanding of what is decisive in the Bible. The Bible is an object of interpretation....The Bible is the book which contains the reports of the events which have happened both in the Old Testament and the New Testament."[1]

Later, as he is dealing with historical relativity, Dr. Cottrell observes that truth can be confused with the understanding of truth. I would merely point out that just as the understanding of the reader is influenced by external factors, such as history and culture, so the understanding of biblical writers can be influenced by their context, even as they perceived the truth of their reality, and even as they were inspired.

The Bible as the Word of God

The discussion of truth and authority as it is presented does not lead to the conclusion that Cottrell draws. He states that where we do not have records of the testimonies of eyewitnesses or the assured results of historical investigation, we must claim that "the Bible is entirely true and thus authoritative because it is the Word—indeed, the very words— of God" (p. 27). Cottrell clarifies his position by offering definitions of revelation and inspiration. While I agree that revelation is the disclosure or making known of that which has previously been unknown, does this definition lead us to Cottrell's statement that "large portions of the Bible are revelation in this sense, i.e., they are words formulated in the very mind of God and disclosed to us through His spokesmen" (p. 28)? If so, then inspiration seems to be limited to the activity of God using a spokesperson or prophet to mediate this revelation to third parties. Thus, "supernatural influence exerted by the Holy Spirit upon prophets and apostles...enabled them to communicate without error or omission those truths, received through revelation or otherwise, that God has deemed necessary for our salvation and service" (p. 29).

When Cottrell notes the reaction of non-conservatives to this understanding of the Bible as the "words of God," these reactions are stated accurately. Yet, I do indeed raise the valid question of whether finite beings can not only understand but record verbatim the thoughts of that which is infinite. Our words themselves are limited in their capacity to communicate. I am reminded of the words of Romans 8:26, which say that, in prayer, the Holy Spirit intercedes for us with sighs too deep for words. Words themselves are unable fully to convey human thought and communication. However, this fact is explained away, from the conservative perspective, with the concept of word revelation.

Cottrell states that the non-conservative tends to overexaggerate the problem of cultural relativity and points to translation as proof that there is seldom any obstacle in communication across cultural boundaries. Inasmuch as I am daily confronted with this issue as I communicate with persons who are of a different cultural context than my own, I am very aware of how culture forms a barrier even when there is the element of *common* language. Different patterns of speech keep us from understanding each other. Translation of language does not always insure translation of intent.

If the moderate view of biblical authority agreed with the line of thinking that is presented, one would indeed come to the conclusion that scripture is authoritative just because it is the word of God. As I affirm God as authority, however, my understanding is (1) that scripture's revelation rests primarily in its disclosure of the person of Jesus Christ and the nature of God, and (2) that inspiration must be understood to include responsive activity as well as passive receptivity toward the Holy Spirit. Therefore this discussion does not lead me to an affirmation of scripture as the Word or words of God. Some would say that this conclusion would even imply that God has in some ways placed in the confines of a human instrument ultimate authority.

The conservative view raises the question of how we are to interpret those passages of scripture that do not express the same message. For example, Paul's teaching on marriage and his doctrine of the cross reveal different levels of perceptions. The message of Amos reflects a somewhat different understanding from that of Hosea. There are fundamental differences in the scales of values held by different people at different times. The writer of the fifty-eighth Psalm prays for the punishment of the wicked, whereas the writer of the fifty-third chapter of Isaiah sees the suffering servant who takes on the sin of the unrighteous as an appropriate model. The portrayal and role of women also come into question. Accepting the concept of verbal inspiration would be to accept (as some have) that God thinks less of women than of men.

When all these points are taken into consideration, it leads one to an understanding that the scriptures, rather than being the actual words of God, are testimonies and confessions of human beings as they understood God's speaking to them. Inasmuch as these testimonies are based upon human experiences and reflections on those experiences, they are subjective. This does not mean that they are inherently erroneous; however, subjectivity does create the environment for error. Nor can we dismiss the fact that the writings were handled by beings who were influenced by their history, social context, and world view. When all this is considered, one must acknowledge that different levels of perception are indeed reflected in scripture.

The Bible as Word of God Established by Reason

In reviewing the arguments that support the scriptures' claim to be of divine origin, we are told that the conservative perspective considers four "Christian evidences": the Bible's unity, fulfilled prophecies, accuracy, and internal consistency. These are presented as self-evident statements of fact, and there seems to be an assumption that everyone draws the same conclusions about these "evidences".

It would have been helpful to have had some discussion of the conservative view of these claims. However, since none is presented, I am led to respond to this section in the form of questions. First, what is the conservative perspective on the unity of the scriptures? Does that perspective simply state that there is a close relationship that exists between the Old and New Testament as two parts of an ongoing drama of revelation, or is that unity defined in terms of its teachings? The claim of unity in the Bible must address the obvious differences in the understanding of the nature and obligations of religion, as well as differences in perspectives of faith and ethics.

Furthermore, what particular prophecies outside of the Christ event are interpreted as fulfilled? How does one define accuracy in light of the variety of expectations that are presented in the Bible? How does one interpret the Synoptics and the gospel of John with a view of internal consistency?[2] Finally, I question whether these evidences are solid enough to lead to the conclusion that is drawn.

Conclusion

I agree with Cottrell's affirmative response to the question, "Is it proper to say that authority can be an attribute of a written document such as the Bible?" (p. xx). However, I do not share the same perspective on that authority. I do begin with the same understanding that ultimate authority rests with God and that the Bible is indeed a means by which the Christian may live under the authority of God. While I affirm the internal authority of scripture, I cannot agree that it can be called the single source of faith and practice. One must also rely upon the continuing revelation of the Holy Spirit, which may indeed confront us outside of the confines of scripture. By saying that we must depend on the "divine truth" as revealed in the Bible or else have no standards allows no room for the creative work of the Holy Spirit that generates revelation.

Even Calvin, who is sometimes seen as a scriptural authoritarian, maintained that the Bible is only authoritative when it is witnessed to by the divine Spirit. The claim for the authority of the scriptures must be properly related to the nature of human experience. There are unique dimensions of human experience that cannot be recorded in literary documents and cannot be seen as only a product of scripture. It has been said that the authority of scripture means that it functions as an arrow to indicate the proper direction, or as a light to illuminate the nature of the situation. This then places a limited authority on the material. 2 Timothy 3:16-17 refers to scripture as inspired and useful, and that usefulness does not hinge only upon a conservative perspective as presented by Dr. Cottrell.

NOTES

¹Paul Tillich, *A History of Christian Thought* (New York: Harper and Row, 1968), p. 309.
²R.C. Briggs, *Interpreting the New Testament Today* (Nashville: Abingdon Press, 1969, 1973), pp. 62-64.

3

The Nature of Biblical Authority: A Moderate Perspective

David M. Scholer

I want to develop my perspective by first making some brief comments on the Christian confession concerning authority and then noting four major concerns about the nature of biblical authority.

The Christian Confession Concerning Authority
1. Ultimate authority belongs to God alone. This perspective is deeply rooted in our theological heritage and traditions and must never be sacrificed to the need and importance of emphasizing the authority of the Bible.
2. The Christian faith at its core is committed to the conviction that God spoke fully and finally (in the last days) in Jesus Christ. Christ is the focus and locus of God's revelation in Christian theology. God's revelation in Christ— as expressed, for example, in John 1:14 ("the Word became

flesh...we have beheld his glory," RSV) and Colossians 2:9 ("For in Christ the whole fulness of deity dwells bodily," RSV)—gives Christ priority in the identification of the Word of God.

3. The Bible as authority is a reflection of and derived from the authority that belongs in the first place to God and to God known in Jesus Christ. This is not to diminish the authority of the Bible, but to set it in its appropriate Christian theological context. The Bible is accepted as authority in the communities of faith (Jewish and Christian) as a confession of faith, the prior condition of which is faith in God and God's self-disclosure in human history, particularly in and among the people of God and, for Christians, in Jesus Christ.

4. The classic Protestant and Reformation affirmations about the Bible's authority expressed in terms such as "final authority," "sufficient authority," "*sola scriptura*," "complete authority," and the like should not be understood as declarations of the Bible over or above God or God in Christ, but as attempts to affirm the Bible as the locus of God's written revelation over against any attempt to shift that locus to some other place, whether that be tradition, reason, or experience.

Major Concerns About the Nature of Biblical Authority

My confession of the authority of the Bible is a product of my understanding of God, God's revelation in Christ, and my acceptance of the church's ancient recognition and confession of the authority of the Bible. I understand that the Bible is accepted as the authority or norm for the life of the church in its theological understandings and in its practice of obedient discipleship. Given that, what is crucial is to reflect on and attempt to define the nature of biblical authority. Here I wish to speak to *four major concerns about the nature of biblical authority*: (1) a perspective on New Testament canon history; (2) the significance of the assertion that the locus of authority is in the text; (3) the hermeneutical dilemma of appropriating biblical authority; and (4) the inadequacies of the late twentieth-century "equation" of biblical authority and biblical inerrancy.

1. *A perspective on New Testament canon history.* Scripture for Jesus and the early church was the Jewish canon. Three observations seem appropriate here. First, scripture (i.e., the Jewish canon) clearly served as authority, not unlike its role in other sectors of Judaism; the difference was the perception of fulfillment in Jesus Christ. The authority of the canon became a hermeneutical issue: What is its historical culmination?

Second, the New Testament writers used, almost exclusively, the Septuagint. Thus issues of authority vis-a-vis the "inerrancy" of the text are predicated on the Septuagint and its traditions and theological argumentation. Third, the oft-used texts in affirming biblical authority such as John 10:35 ("Scripture cannot be broken," RSV) and 2 Timothy 3:16 ("all scripture is inspired by God," RSV) refer in their context and intent only to the Jewish canon; thus it is only by theological extension when the Christian faith affirms that the New Testament can be included here in any sense.

The early church began and grew on the basis of Jesus' life, death, and resurrection, the guiding of the Holy Spirit, and the ministry of the apostolic band and those added to it, but these occurred without the historical reality of a New Testament. Moreover, the New Testament canon—the acceptance of these twenty-seven texts and *no* others—is not itself a datum of revelation; i.e., no inspired, authoritative text defines the New Testament canon itself. Thus, the New Testament canon emerged within the history of the early church. In this sense, church precedes canon. It is true, however, that the early church itself names the New Testament canon as its authoritative standard. The concept of a New Testament canon emerged in the period C.E. 150-175, perhaps with Marcion. As noted by Eusebius,[1] Melito (ca. C.E. 175) calls the Jewish canon the Old Testament and Tertullian (ca. C.E. 200) may be the first explicitly to use the terminology "New Testament."[2] However, this New Testament was not the same as the twenty-seven-book New Testament, even though here was considerable overlap.

We accept the New Testament canon as the authoritative Bible by faith in God's providential work in and through the early church. We may speak of the inherent qualities (e.g., apostolicity) of the books that comprise the New Testament, but that is an *ex post facto* judgment given the realities of canon history. These are hardly the only documents that claimed apostolic character and/or truthfulness. In fact, we ascribe authority to the New Testament because of its consensus emergence in the second-to-fourth-century C.E. church—believing, of course, that the process embodies the providential work of God.

These observations may suggest something of the contingent character of biblical authority. Tertullian, perhaps the first to use the explicit New Testament designation consciously, provides a window or paradigm for understanding the concept of the New Testament and its authority. First, note Tertullian's intriguing statement: "For without scripture there can be no heresy."[3] Here Tertullian, who understands the New Testament to be the authority, has a functional triad of text (the New Testament), tradition (*regula fidei*), and the interpretive struggle and options. Thus, Tertullian says,

> arguments about scripture achieve nothing but a stomachache or a headache....They rely on passages which they have put together in a false context or fastened on because of their ambiguity....It follows that we must not appeal to Scripture and we must not contend on ground where victory is impossible....For only where the true Christian teaching and faith are evident will the true Scriptures, the true interpretations, and all the true Christian traditions be found.[4]

In other words, the actuality of conferring scriptural authority is an interplay of tradition (the rule of faith; or for us, an orthodox structure of belief), scripture, and interpretive struggle.

This interpretive struggle concerned Tertullian on both the right and the left, as illustrated in his *On Baptism* 10-16.[5] For example, consider the question: Jesus did not baptize anyone; thus, what is the authority for baptism?

To his left, against the Cainites (a gnostic sect denying water baptism), Tertullian argues from the "standing rule" and against the heretics' "over-precise or even audacious" use (or misuse) of scripture. To his right, against those who argue that Jesus baptized his apostles with the waves in the boat in the storm (Matt. 8:24, etc.), Tertullian says that is "obviously far-fetched." The entire section, *On Baptism* 10-16, shows that the authority of scripture functioned only within a hermeneutical-interpretive debate and using claims to frameworks that protected or guaranteed the truth. If Tertullian's insight is valid that "without Scripture there can be no heresy," repeated in our time in Ernst Kasemann's dictum that the canon may not constitute only the unity of the church but its diversity as well,[6] then we can see that the emergence of the New Testament canon does affirm the New Testament and Bible as authoritative. But that authority is functional, and is appropriated only through the larger contexts of faith and of the interpretive-hermeneutical struggle.

2. *The locus of authority is in the text; the Bible is the authority.*[7] There are several contexts for this affirmation. First, the Bible *is* authoritative in its words; it does not only become authoritative nor only witness to authority. Second, the text is the locus of authority over against those views that place the locus of authority outside the text, either in the traditions before the texts (e.g., oral sources; reconstructing the "historical/real" Jesus; etc.) or in those who see the locus of authority in the reader (some types of reader-response theory) or the reader's experience (e.g., various typologies of liberation and feminist theologies). I do not mean to be naive in claiming that it is easy to identify the text's intention, but it *is* possible to achieve objective interpretation (more on the difficulties, though, below). This position, I contend, respects the integrity of texts and provides a meaningful point of reference for a concept of authority.

However, there are several major implications of this commitment, a commitment that can actually be understood as a "conservative" commitment on the nature of biblical authority. The first concerns the historical particularity of texts. Every document in the Bible is shaped by the setting in which it was produced. There are no texts that are not culturally conditioned. This is not to say that texts cannot at the same time bear divine revelation and speak with divine authority. It is to say that, in fact, all biblical texts were written by real persons to real persons in real historical-cultural contexts. I do not believe the evangelical tradition—with which I identify—has yet understood this sort of narrow, historical particularity. Evangelicals have refuted Christological docetism, but have never truly eliminated docetism from their view of the Bible. We somehow hope that the biblical texts were not touched by the culture in which they were produced. Yet cultural factors do not minimize biblical authority any more than recognizing Jesus' full humanity minimizes his authority. It is simply the way it is. It does mean that appropriating the authority of the Bible becomes an interpretative struggle.

Closely related to the historical particularity of the texts is the *diversity* among biblical texts. There is a place to talk about the unity of the New Testament—it is certainly tied to the affirmation that Jesus Christ is the final and full revelation of God—but the reality of diversity remains. The so-called "left" is prone to construe diversity as contradiction and consequently eliminate texts; the so-called "right" is prone to obliterate diversity by predetermined harmonizations and consequently eliminate texts. In either case, parts of the Bible are ignored or even rejected, in one case rather openly and in the other case rather subtly or even unconsciously. The reality of the Bible should be likened to a patchwork quilt of many colors and individually patterned squares that displays its total beautiful unity by its very diversity. The Bible is neither a quilt of one color and one pattern throughout nor a collection of unsewn patches. We must let the Bible gloriously speak; and part of its "glory" consists in its multifaceted diversity. All facile and falsely motivated attempts to "harmonize" texts that violate their meaning and power must be rejected. The diversity of the Bible is certainly one of the means through which the Bible has the potential for continuous relevance and application to various times and situations. To resist this is to undercut the real, functional authority of the Bible and the very mode in which God actually communicated in scripture.

Biblical authority is not diminished by recognizing its historical particularity or its diversity. These recognitions, in fact, take seriously that the locus of authority is in the biblical texts themselves. Space does not allow the development of examples but we may point to two areas for consideration by way of example. First, the New Testament canon has four gospels; they differ, and the church has always been embarrassed by this—from Tatian to Augustine to evangelical-bred harmonizations to the student who said to me, "God would never give us four gospels!" Second, consider the historical particularity related to texts about women and sexuality in the New Testament: the example of 1 Timothy 5:3-16 regarding widows and the failure of those committed to "biblical authority" to follow it as they have argued 1 Timothy 2:11-12 should be followed.

3. *The hermeneutical dilemma of appropriating biblical authority.* The eternal God opted for self-revelation within the only setting we could comprehend: the historically conditioned particularity of human life. If it is not irreverent to say it, our hermeneutical dilemma is but a reflection of the eternal, transcendent God's revelatory dilemma. And while the Bible is the authority in the church, authority is appropriated only by interpretation and through interpreters; there is no escape from the interpretive or hermeneutical dilemma, there is no "first horizon" place of refuge. Thus all biblical interpretation is socially located, individually skewed, and ecclesiastically and theologically conditioned.

Hence, without abandoning the conviction of biblical authority or the affirmation that the locus of meaning is in the text, the fact is that the Bible is appropriated only and always by us and other persons. Now some, perhaps especially strong biblical inerrantists, hope that a strong commitment to biblical authority somehow guarantees clarity—objective, correct, and authoritative interpretations of texts. Alas, the reality is that meaning is found somewhere in the inextricable interplay between the coercion of the text itself and the significance or function of the text accorded to it by the interpreter or interpreting community. The locus of meaning as experienced is in practice found in an individual interpreter, a particular community or a specific ecclesiastical or theological tradition. This complex interplay is a hermeneutical reality and predicament from which there is no escape.

In this connection one ought to feel the force of what I call the "all and only" challenge once given to me as a Protestant by my Roman Catholic New Testament colleague, Raymond E. Brown. He said: "Show me a Protestant who really accepts all of the Bible and who really accepts *only* the Bible." Indeed, our hermeneutical dilemma is genuine.

How does one prevent the "subjectivity" of the interpreters from overwhelming the "objectivity" of historically located texts? This can be done—even within the interplay of the "two horizons"—by taking seriously the coercion of the text, by taking seriously the contributions of the believing community past and present, by an awareness of the factors that condition interpretation, and by a commitment to the ongoing tasks of continuous exegesis and understanding biblical texts in the life of the church. A commitment to biblical authority does not eliminate the need for ongoing interpretation; the static view (e.g., Charles Hodge who said proudly: "I am not afraid to say that a new idea never originated in this Seminary"[8]) falsely identifies "my" interpretation with the authority that belongs only to the text itself. These realities should never allow a person to accuse or charge another with denying biblical authority when what is at issue is the conception and acknowledgment of our common hermeneutical predicament.

    4. The inadequacies of the late twentieth-century "equation" of biblical authority and biblical inerrancy. Because the "moderate perspective" I represent claims a sense of biblical authority with the same intention regarding the Bible as conservatives (though not understood that way by conservatives), it is important to identify the problems with the concept of inerrancy as developed in the second half of the twentieth century, particularly in the United States. These problems have clouded or perverted the sound concept of biblical authority that has been the more general heritage of the Christian tradition throughout much of the history of the church.

First, inerrancy imposes expectations upon the text (asserting what the text must be) without recognizing the text in fact and the actual character of the text itself. Inerrancy usually involves some type of static, monolithic, one-dimensional relationship between God and the Bible. This denies the dynamic and complex character of authorial intent, the nature of human language, and the fact of historically particularized texts.

Moreover, inerrancy confuses or tends to confuse the upholding or preservation of the inerrancy position, seen as the only legitimate defense of biblical authority, with the issue of the interpretation of a text. In other words, an interpretation that differs from that of a particular inerrantist is too often or too readily seen not as a difference of interpretation but as a denial of biblical authority. Relatedly, inerrancy also falsely assumes that commitment to inerrancy (and thus to biblical authority) safeguards doctrinal or orthodox purity. It does not. Inerrancy assumes a larger philosophical framework that is not true to experience. Inerrancy is not necessary, for the dynamic consistency of experience makes it clear that a completely rational, ordered universe as a conceptual framework is not possible; there are inconsistencies and irreconcilable data. Inerrancy pushes beyond experienced reality. With high investment in static, monolithic, and propositional facticity, one error, or even one perceived variance, is seen or can be seen to call into question the truth and thus God. Inerrancy is, seen on its own terms, "all or nothing." But, if one allows for the complexity and ambiguity of human experience, language, and particularity, such capitulations are hardly necessary. By analogy that same framework, it would seem to me, would require one in the face of evil and injustice in the world and throughout its history to conclude that God is not both all-powerful and all-good. But we affirm in the Christian faith that, in spite of the insoluble problems of evil and suffering, God is all-powerful and all-good. Scriptural variety, tensions, difficulties, and incongruencies do not at all necessarily question God or truth. My adherence to biblical authority and to God are not captive to the fact that reality is so complex that it transcends my ability to domesticate it.

Inerrantists have misread the history of the church's commitment to biblical authority by seeing in it a uniform, centuries-long commitment to inerrancy as presently conceived. To take but one example in the early church, Justin Martyr's and Augustine's affirmations and defenses of coherence and agreement of all the Bible (what inerrantists would call inerrancy in their terms) come out of radically different assumptions about the structure and nature of reality, authorial intent, and hermeneutic resolution than does late-twentieth-century inerrancy. I refer here, for example, to Justin's overenthusiastic fulfillment interpretations of the Old Testament or Augustine's allegorical resolutions of gospel difficulties.

Inerrancy also makes or presumes the issue to be more important than it is. Far more critical than inerrancy in the matter of the authority of the Bible are at least two other items: responsible interpretation and faithful obedience!

Consider an inerrantist approach to the issue found in Acts 7:16, where Stephen's speech is reported as saying that Abraham bought a tomb from the sons of Hamor in Shechem. Now according to the Old Testament it was Jacob who did this (Josh. 24:32); Abraham bought a tomb in Hebron (Gen. 23:16; 49:29-32; 50:13). Certain typologies of response are possible. E. Haenchen claims the report is somehow "confused."[9] F.F. Bruce believes it to be "telescoped."[10] G.L. Archer says Abraham *"must"* have previously bought the Shechem field and Jacob repurchased it, and that this is "altogether logical." For, he writes, "Stephen was undoubtedly aware of a reliable oral tradition that Abraham had in fact done so, even though the written record of the Old Testament had omitted [the] transaction."[11]

So much for *sola scriptura*! Instead we see the "counsel of desperation"—a rational defense of doctrine apart from the text of the Bible itself. The fact that responsible interpretation must accept is that Acts 7:16 is not congruent with the Old Testament. This does not destroy or deny the authority of the Bible. Rather the authority is enhanced by integrity. Authority is not preserved by calling it "telescoping" or by positing an addition to the Old Testament.

Conclusion

The Bible is the authority for the life of the church. Its authority is dependent upon the fact that it is *God's* word and that it *witnesses to Jesus Christ* as the full and final revelation of God. Thus, its authority is sufficient and true.

The Bible's very composition constitutes a hermeneutical predicament that calls for responsible interpretation. It is in this commitment that there is integrity to the claim of biblical authority. The commitment to the Bible as authority is crucial for continuity with the tradition of the church and for the appropriate point of reference in matters of faith and life, but functional authority comes only in the interpretive process— the dynamic interplay between text and interpreter.

Finally, it is only in this commitment *augmented by the response of faithful obedience* that biblical authority has any ultimate integrity, ultimate meaning, and eternal value.

NOTES

[1] Melito, cited in Eusebius, Ecclesiastical *History* 4.26.13-14, in F.F. Bruce, *The Canon of Scripture* (Downer's Grove: InterVarsity Press, 1988), pp. 70f.

[2] Tertullian, *Against Praxeas* 15, in F.F. Bruce, *The Canon of Scripture, op cit*, p. 181.

[3] Tertullian, *Prescriptions Against Heretics*, tr. S.L. Greenslade, *Early Latin Theology*, Library of Christian Classics, vol. 5 (Philadelphia: Westminster Press, 1956), p. 60.

[4] *Ibid.*, pp. 42f.

[5] Tertullian, *On Baptism*, tr. Earnest Evans, *Tertullian's Homily on Baptism* (London: S.P.C.K., 1964).

[6] Ernst Kasemann, "The Canon of the New Testament and the Unity of the Church," in *Essays on New Testament Themes: Studies in Biblical The-*

68

ology, vol. 4 (London: S.C.M. Press, 1964), pp. 95-107.

⁷ The remainder of this article draws heavily on four previous works of mine: "Unreasonable Thoughts on the State of Biblical Hermeneutics," *American Baptist Quarterly* 2 (1983), pp. 134-141; "Issues in Biblical Interpretation," *Evangelical Quarterly* 60 (1988), pp. 5-22; "Feminist Hermeneutics and Evangelical Biblical Interpretation," *Journal of the Evangelical Theological Society* 30 (1987), pp. 407-420; "How Can Divine Revelation Be So Human? *Daughters of Sarah* 15/3 (May/June 1989), pp. 11-15.

⁸ Quoted in Mark A. Noll, *The Princeton Theology: 1812-1921* (Grand Rapids: Baker, 1983), p. 38.

⁹Ernst Haenchen, *The Acts of the Apostles: A Commentary* (Philadelphia: Westminster Press, 1971), p. 280.

¹⁰F.F. Bruce, *The Book of Acts*, rev. ed., *The New International Commentary on the New Testament* (Grand Rapids: Eerdmans, 1988), p. 137, note 35.

¹¹Gleason L. Archer, *Encyclopedia of Bible Difficulties* (Grand Rapids: Zondervan, 1982), pp. 379-381.

A Conservative Response

Richard D. Land

I am a Southern Baptist both by background and inclination. I grew up in a typically conservative Southern Baptist church where it was assumed without question that the Bible had "God for its author, salvation for its end, and truth, without any mixture of error, for its matter."[1] Indeed, at the outset of this century, J.M. Frost, founder of the Southern Baptist Convention's Sunday School Board, which produces educational curriculum for the churches, declared,

> We accept the scriptures as an all-sufficient and infallible rule of faith and practice, and insist upon the absolute inerrancy and sole authority of the Word of God. We recognize at this point no room for division, either of practice or belief....More and more we must come to feel as the deepest and mightiest power of our

conviction that a "thus saith the Lord" is the end of all controversy.[2]

This was "the rock" from whence I was "hewn" and "the pit" from whence I was "digged" (Isa. 51:1, KJV). However, the church and the tradition of which I was a part was not caught up in the confessional rigidity or legalistic behavioral patterns often found in more readily identifiable fundamentalist traditions or denominations.

The Wheaton College historian, Mark Noll, in discussing the Christian tradition concerning the nature of biblical authority, concluded forthrightly:

> Most Christians in most churches since the founding of Christianity have believed in the inerrancy of the Bible. Or at least they have believed that the scriptures are inspired by God, and so are the words of eternal life. The term *inerrancy* was not common until the nineteenth century. But the conviction that God communicates in Scripture a revelation of himself and of his deeds, and that this revelation is entirely truthful, has always been the common belief of most Catholics, most Protestants, most Orthodox, and even most of the sects of the fringe of Christianity.[3]

The position Noll espouses is very clear. For most Christians, in most places, in most traditions, at most times, the Bible has been understood and accepted as "entirely truthful."

A concerted attempt has been made in recent years to revive earlier attempts to make the nineteenth-century "Princeton theologians" the progenitors of a far more elaborate doctrine of inerrancy than that which existed in earlier epochs of Christian history up to and including the sixteenth- and seventeenth-century reformers. The leading recent proponents of such a view have been Jack Rogers and Donald McKim in *The Authority and Interpretation of the Bible: An Historical Approach* (New York: Harper & Row, 1979).

The "Rogers-McKim Proposal," as it is often known in historical circles, clearly seems to be accepted by Scholer when he asserts that the "'equation' of biblical authority and biblical inerrancy" has "clouded or perverted the sound concept of biblical authority that has been the more general heritage of the Christian tradition throughout much of the history of the church" (pp. 64f.).

Numerous scholars have examined the evidence and have found themselves agreeing with Noll's viewpoint and rejecting that espoused by Rogers-McKim and supported by Scholer. John Woodbridge's exhaustive examination of the "Rogers-McKim Proposal" revealed severe methodological and evidential shortcomings.[4] I fully agree with Noll's assessment that Woodbridge's "more conservative position seems clearly stronger in the exact matter under consideration."[5]

In other words, on the narrow historical question of what was believed in most places at most times in the patristic period, in the Middle Ages, in the Reformation, and up to and including the nineteenth century, those arguing for a more conservative understanding of inerrancy as the prevailing view are supported by the overwhelming preponderance of the evidence. Brunner acknowledged that the "doctrine of Verbal Inspiration was already known to pre-Christian Judaism and was probably also taken over by Paul and the rest of the Apostles." [6]

Yet, as Noll and Lake both have noted, the question of what our Christian forebears believed about the Bible does not answer the question of whether they were correct. A second separate question is, "Were they accurate in their assessment of the Bible?"

To answer the first question affirmatively does not provide an automatically affirmative answer to the second. Especially is this true for those of us who stand in the free-church tradition, where tradition is supposed to play a subordinate role. Baptists and others in the free-church tradition have often assumed inaccurately that, since they theoretically are not bound by their tradition, they do not possess one. We do have a long and proud tradition. Hopefully, we view it as instructive, rather than as binding or merely informational in nature. We in the free-church tradition must seek to determine historical truth while understanding that it provides no conclusive answers in searching for answers to contemporary doctrinal questions.

Near the beginning of his paper, Dr. Scholer makes a point to which I want to return. He asserts that the fundamental Christian understanding about authority is that "ultimate authority belongs to God alone" and that "God spoke fully and finally...in Jesus Christ" and that this "gives Christ priority in the identification of the Word of God." Thus, the Bible's authority is "derived from the authority that belongs in the first place to God and to God known in Jesus Christ" (pp. 57f.).

I agree. My questions to Dr. Scholer are, "How does he know that? How does he know who God is? How does he know who Jesus Christ is?" For those of us in the evangelical tradition, we believe that most of what can be known objectively, non-experientially about Jesus, we learn from the Bible. In fact, Scholer cites John. 1:14 and Colossians 2:9 in making his assertions about Jesus.

What recourse other than acceptance of New Testament revelation do we have? Unless we take Bultmann's position that the New Testament does not tell us much about Jesus, but rather what the first-century community of faith believed about Jesus, what reliable source do we possess other than the New Testament record? Indeed, the Jesus that can be known and is knowable is the Jesus that is revealed to us in scripture.

At this point I want to quote a theologian to whom I personally owe a great debt, Carl F. H. Henry. In his response to this question in a chapel service several years ago, Henry raised salient points.

Nobody has ever been able to come up with a truly objective principle for approaching scripture and designing within it any tracks which are considered unreliable. Whenever the principle of unreliability so called is introduced, it soon gathers into its grip, if it is consistently applied, much more than the scholar usually intended. I know that it is very attractive to say that after all for Christians, Jesus Christ is the supreme and final revelation of God and it is to Jesus that we ought to appeal.

I am certainly sympathetic to that. I feel the sting of the argument when people say that if the living God is supreme and final authority over human life, we ought not to have secondary authorities to whom or to which we ascribe absolute finality.[7]

When we begin speaking about the Bible as having "derived authority," it is critically important to remember that God is unknowable, and Christ is unknowable in any objective sense apart from an authoritative word from God in the Bible.

God has given us a special revelation in scripture. He has taken the initiative to reveal Himself to us far more completely than through general revelation. He has chosen to reveal Himself in a manner comprehensible to us as human beings. Consequently, even as fallen and sinful human beings, we can, with the Holy Spirit's aid, know God. We can learn what He expects of us, and we are enabled to comprehend and to obey His instruction and to receive His wisdom and to experience His blessing.

This special revelation of God is given to us through a scripture, an "inspired" word from God. "By inspiration we mean that supernatural influence of the Holy Spirit upon the scripture writers which rendered their writings an accurate record of the revelation or which resulted in what they wrote actually being the Word of God."[8]

That does not mean that He did not employ the personalities of the writers. It does not mean that He did not employ their life experiences. In fact, the apostle Paul suggests that God set him apart and consecrated him before he was born to be exactly who he was when he began to use him to reveal precisely what He wanted revealed (Gal. 1:15).

Dr. Scholer emphasizes the Bible's diversity of human authors and their cultural particularity. This does not present the problem to the inerrantist that he seems to suppose. Many years ago B.B. Warfield addressed this issue. He was challenged by critics who asserted that the humanity of the biblical writers would "condition and qualify" the writings they produced and would make impossible "a pure word of God."[9] The critics reasoned that just as sunlight is stained by the tint of the glass in a stained glass window, so the work of God would be distorted and discolored by the humanity of the writer. Warfield responded by asking his own questions:

> But what if this personality has itself been formed by God into precisely the personality it is, for the express purpose of communicating to the word given through it just the coloring which it gives it? What if the colors of the stained-glass window have been designed by the architect for the express purpose of giving to the light that floods the cathedral precisely the tone and quality it receives from them?[10]

Warfield's point is well taken. In the inerrantist view, God is also the designer of the stained glass window. The individual mosaics that are the human aspects and facets of the biblical writers are the individual, differently tinted hues that compose the design God wanted us to see.

Scholer seems to think that such human diversity in both the writers and the "historical particularity" of the biblical texts are terribly troubling to inerrantists. I, with many other inerrantists, am willing to acknowledge that the text is touched by its historical and cultural particularity. But I am unwilling to accept that it has been tainted by such contact anymore than the person of Christ was tainted, rather than touched, by the Incarnation. I believe Scholer is also mistaken in attributing to inerrantists such excessive love for harmonization of the four gospels. I am an inerrantist. I, and many other inerrantists, preach the reasons why God gave us four gospels, not one. Many inerrantists believe that in their diversity they illustrate various facets of the purposes of Jesus that God intended for us to understand. The four gospels produced four different portraits of the Savior.

Now, given the confusion that continues to arise over what is meant by inerrancy, I believe it would be helpful to furnish a brief definition. "Inerrancy means that when all facts are known, the scriptures in their original autographs and properly interpreted will be shown to be wholly true in everything that they affirm, whether that has to do with doctrine or morality or with the social, physical or life sciences."[11]

Another point at which I find Scholer's terminology disturbing is when he speaks of the interpreter "appropriating the authority of the Bible." I do not believe that we can ever, or should ever try to, appropriate scripture's authority. No one's interpretation must ever be allowed to stand on a parallel with the authority of the Bible.

I would also reject Scholer's analogy that God's revelational dilemma in how He was going to relate to us parallels the dilemma of the interpreter because God faced a dilemma based upon our limitations—not any limitations of His which in the analogy would be extrapolated to the limitations of the text.

In closing, there are three additional points I want to raise. Scholer rejects the so-called "slippery slope" argument espoused by many inerrantists, which says that if there are any mistakes and errors admitted, then all will be lost. John Wesley articulated the concept when he said, "If there be any mistakes in the Bible, there may well be a thousand. If there be one falsehood in that book, it did not come from the God of truth."[12] I agree with Woodbridge's perspective that the "slippery slope" is too mechanistic, too inexorable, too deterministic, and too contrary to some historical experience to serve as the most useful analogy.[13]

Perhaps it would be better to adopt the approach put forward by Millard Erickson that "history is the laboratory in which theology tests its ideas" and that the trend in history for abandonment of the "complete trustworthiness of the Bible is a very serious step," with often severe consequences.[14]

Rather than a "false in one, false in all" argument, it is more a "false in one, uncertain in all" tendency.[15]

When one looks at the historical record, one finds that those who have abandoned a high view of scripture—those people, those institutions, those traditions—have far more often than not found it very difficult to sustain a high view of authority and doctrinal orthodoxy. However, in some cases it has been done, and the movement has not always been in one direction.

I would like to suggest perhaps a better analogy, Woodbridge's "hinge."

According to this analogy, a door represents the Bible's intended teachings; a doorframe represents "what is the case," that is the truth of the matter in those areas where the Bible makes positive affirmations (about doctrine, ethics, history, geography...) The hinge represents an individual's or an institution's evaluation of the scriptures.

Until the end of the seventeenth century the vast majority of Europeans having the door as the doorframe with a very sturdy hinge: the Bible in what it intends to teach is exactly "what is the case." The pin of inerrancy gave this hinge its exceptional quality.[16]

Since the seventeenth century many substitute hinges have been tried, with varying degrees of success. None has proven as durable or as sturdy as inerrancy. It should be noted that this is an agreement from consequence, and such arguments are never conclusive.

Dr. Scholer also argues in his paper that inerrantists tend "to confuse the upholding or preservation of the inerrancy position...with the issue of the interpretation of a text" (p. 65). I do not think that is necessarily true, and I do not think it is even mostly true, especially among those writing and working in these areas from inerrantist perspective such as James Packer, Carl F.H. Henry, Kenneth Kantzer, and Millard Erickson. It has been my experience and observation that most inerrantists know the difference between a question of interpretation such as the nature of church and eschatology and a question of biblical authority in the espousal of universalism or the denial of the clear teaching in the first chapter of Romans concerning homosexuality.

I also want to address Dr. Scholer's admonition "never [to] allow a person to accuse or charge another with denying biblical authority when what is at issue is the conception and acknowledgment of our common hermeneutical predicament" (p. xx). In most cases I would agree in that I would be very reluctant, as would most inerrantists, to accuse Scholer of denying biblical authority, or even of consciously undermining it. He clearly takes the Bible very seriously. Inerrantists such as myself would still want to point out, if necessary, some of the inherent dangers they may perceive in some of the approaches to scripture taken by those who see themselves as holding a high view of biblical authority. Also, I am a little concerned by the inclusiveness of "never" in his statement. I would like to hear Scholer address the issue of how someone would have to treat the scripture before he would accuse them of denying biblical authority.

In closing, let me stress once again that what the church had believed is a different question than whether the church was right to believe as it did. Once again, arguments from consequences are never conclusive, but in sufficient number, they do make cause for concern. I am concerned about the future of evangelical Christianity. And I suspect that the success and vitality of evangelicalism over the past third of the twentieth century finds one of its most important sources in the certainty that it carries in its heart, mind, and hand a sure and a certain word from God. Such is a certainty that creates confidence, conquers confusion, and dissipates dizziness.

78

NOTES

[1] *The Baptist Faith and Message* (Nashville: The Sunday School Board, 1963), "Article I. The Scriptures," p. 7.

[2] J.M. Frost ed., *Baptist: Why and Why Not* (Nashville: Sunday School Board of the Southern Baptist Convention, 1900), p. 12.

[3] Mark Noll, "A Brief History of Inerrancy, Mostly in America," in *The Proceedings of the Conference on Biblical Inerrancy, 1987* (Nashville: Broadman Press, 1987), pp. 9f., citing John D. Woodbridge, *Biblical Authority: A Critique of the Rogers-McKim Proposal* (Grand Rapids: Zondervan, 1982). This last point, that inerrancy was the belief of sects on "the fringe of Christianity" supports Scholer's contention that a belief in inerrancy is not a vaccination against heretical or cultic belief. However, most inerrantists would question whether many inerrantists ever thought that it would, or did, guarantee orthodoxy.

[4] John D. Woodbridge, *Biblical Authority: A Critique of the Rogers-McKim Proposal* (Grand Rapids: Zondervan, 1982).

[5] Mark A. Noll, *Between Faith and Criticism: Evangelicals, Scholarship, and the Bible in America* (San Francisco: Harper & Row, 1986), p. 218.

[6] Emil Brunner, *The Christian Doctrine of God*. Vol. 1 of *Dogmatics*, trans. Olive Wyon (Philadelphia: Westminster Press, 1950), p. 107. For further evidence that such a position is historically correct, see the following:

Bruce Vawter, *Biblical Inspiration* (Philadelphia: Westminster Press, 1972), pp. 132f. Vawter's conclusion is made more compelling by his own lack of sympathy with such views theologically.

J.N.D. Kelly, *Early Christian Doctrines*, rev. ed. (New York: Harper & Row, 1978), pp. 61f.

Geoffrey Bromiley, "The Church Fathers and Holy Scripture," in *Scripture and Truth*, ed. D.A. Carson and John D. Woodbridge (Grand Rapids: Zondervan, 1983), p. 206.

Richard Lovelace, "Inerrancy: Some Historical Perspectives," in *Inerrancy and Common Sense*, ed. Roger R. Nicole and J. Ramsey Michaels (Grand Rapids: Baker Book House, 1980), p. 20, quoting Augustine, Letter 82.3.

Hans Kung, *Infallible? An Enquiry* (London: Collins, 1972) pp. 173f.

Karl Barth, *Church Dogmatics*, ed. G.W. Bromiley and T.F. Torrance (Edinburgh: T.&T. Clark, 1936-1969), I/2, pp. 517, 520.

John Warwick Montgomery, "Lessons from Luther on the Inerrancy of Holy Writ," and J.I. Packer, "Calvin's View of Scripture," in *God's Inerrant Word*, ed. John Warwick Montgovery (Minneapolis: Bethany Fellowship, 1974) pp. 63-94 and 95-114 respectively. Cf. also Carl F.H. Henry, *God, Revelation, and Authority* (Waco: Word Books, 1979), vol. IV, pp. 368-384.

Martin Luther, *The Works of Martin Luther* (Philadelphia: United Lutheran Publishing House, 1915-1932), vol. V, 147.

Dr. Martin Luther's *Small Catechism* (St. Louis: Concordia Publishing House, 1943, slightly revised 1965), p. 41.

John Calvin, *Institutes* (Grand Rapids: Eerdmans, 1975) I, p. 71. Cf. Woodbridge, *op. cit.*, pp. 49-67 for detailed discussion of Luther's and Calvin's views on the authority of Scripture.
Kirsop Lake, *The Religion of Yesterday and Tomorrow* (Boston: Houghton, 1926), p. 61.
[7] Carl F.H. Henry, Chapel, Criswell College, Dallas, Texas, April 22, 1982.
[8] Millard J. Erickson, *Christian Theology* (Grand Rapids: Baker Book House, 1983-1985), p. 199. See also pp. 227-233.
[9] B. B. Warfield, *The Inspiration and Authority of the Bible*, ed. Samuel G. Craig (Philadelphia: Presbyterian and Reformed Publishing, 1967), pp. 155, 165.
[10] *Ibid.*, p. 165.
[11] Paul D. Feinberg, "The Meaning of Inerrancy," in Norman L. Geisler, *Inerrancy* (Grand Rapids: Zondervan, 1979), p. 294. Cf. *Ibid.*, pp. 294 ff., for additional explanation and qualification. Cf. also Erickson, *op. cit.*, pp. 233ff.
[12] John Wesley, *Journal* VI, p. 117, quoted in James Montgomery Boice, *Does Inerrancy Matter?* (Oakland: International Council on Biblical Inerrancy, 1979), p. 28.
[13] John D. Woodbridge, "History's 'Lessons' and Biblical Inerrancy," *Trinity Journal* 6 (Spring, 1977), pp. 73ff.
[14] Erickson, *op.cit.*, p. 226, citing Richard Lovelace, "Inerrancy: Some Historical Perspectives" in *Inerrancy and Common Sense*, pp. 26-36.
[15] Erickson, *op.cit.*, citing Dewey Beegle, *Scripture, Tradition, and Infallibility* (Grand Rapids: Eerdmans, 1973), pp. 219-222, 227.
[16] Woodbridge, "History's 'Lessons,'" pp. 83f.

A Liberal Response

Charles W. Allen

I want to preface my response by noting a peculiarity in the makeup of this section's group. All three of us are Baptists of some sort. David Scholer, our designated "moderate," is an American Baptist; Richard Land, a Southern Baptist, is supposed to offer a conservative response. So far the labels may fit people's expectations. You do not expect an American Baptist to be as liberal as, say, a Disciple, but you do expect him to be more "open" (whatever that means) than a Southern Baptist. But I, too, the liberal respondent, am a *Southern* Baptist. In any case, it looks as if denominational labels do not always tell you what to expect.

The same goes for other labels—such as conservative, moderate or liberal, as William Placher has pointed out. They probably capture some of the differences that would help distinguish the three of us from one another, and as long as that's all they are intended to do, I suppose I can go ahead and embrace the "L"-word. But then I would want to include lots of other people who call themselves something else—revisionist, postliberal, postmodern, postanalytic. (You can tell from all the "post-something-or-others" that there are a lot of people around these days who are tired of options they've been stuck with but are not sure what else to hope for yet.)

To fulfill my duties as a respondent I looked for something with which to disagree in Scholer's paper. But if we're going to disagree I would like it to be over something important, and that is not so easy to carry out. I am sure, for example, that we do not see eye to eye on how historically accurate the gospels probably are, but I am less sure of how far we would disagree over how accurate the gospels might *need* to be in order to preserve the integrity of a Christian witness. We also draw different conclusions about the philosophical literature on hermeneutics, but again I am not sure how instructive it would be to pursue that, especially since I suspect that we tend to agree on the same basic points and differ mainly over when to introduce them. I do wonder what becomes of the claim that "the locus of authority is in the text" if we place it next to the deconstructionists' claim that there is no world outside of some text. And of course we may have serious differences on the nature of God and certainly of freedom, but I do not want to pursue that. Maybe I am supposed to argue that Scholer should either join us liberals or cut bait—an argument conservatives might want to make as well. Or perhaps I am supposed to suggest that, for all practical purposes, he already has joined the liberals. Again, conservatives might concur.

Much depends here on how liberals are portrayed. Luke Johnson has been assigned the official task of presenting a liberal understanding of scriptural authority. I think the position he stakes out—a position I find very promising—definitely qualifies as liberal. I want now to explain why my position would also qualify as liberal, and while obviously I see some convergence between the position I will stake out and Johnson's, they are hardly identical. In terms of the jargon I mentioned earlier, Johnson probably considers his approach "postliberal," while I would call mine "revisionist." In fact, much of what I find congenial in Johnson's canonical approach is its perhaps unintended proximity to David Tracy's model of a "working canon." But William Placher has recently observed in an excellent book that revisionists and postliberals are both trying to say the right things—right, that is, by *our* lights—but we do still say them differently and it is still not clear how important those differences are. I think Scholer and I are also trying to say the right things, and are not quite sure what our different ways of saying them finally amount to, *except*, perhaps, that we feel most at home with different sorts of colleagues. We will return to that after I sketch what seems to be involved in identifying oneself as a liberal.

I call myself a Christian because the Christian witness to God's good news in Jesus Christ seems to claim me just as insistently as anything else I take to be true. As a result, I also fundamentally trust the overall traditioning process that makes that witness available to me today. Scripture plays a pivotal role in that process, but so do post-canonical traditions down to the present, where of course the use of scripture is also pivotal. I call myself a *liberal* Christian, broadly speaking, because I see no need to exempt any part of that traditioning process from the usual perplexities—the errors and atrocities—of human history. Therefore, my trust in the process as a whole does not rule out a healthy dose of suspicion as well, extending all the way to scripture itself. I see no reason to resist the conclusion that the writers of both testaments frequently lost track of the message they were called to proclaim. That is, after all, what their message leads me to expect of them. Liberals are often accused of passing judgment on scripture from what they presume to be a superior external standpoint—enlightenment rationalism, for example. I think that attitude is better described as modernism, however, and its most fashionable period was probably the eighteenth century, before the likes of Schleiermacher, though of course one still finds examples of it today. Like the belief in inerrancy, modernism is an attempt to avoid the perplexities of all human history, only instead of exempting the Bible from those perplexities it tries to exempt some currently fashionable world-view. Now, I am not alluding here to Bultmann or Tillich or process theologians. Such thinkers know better than to settle for such a simplistic escape, at least most of the time. Indeed, liberal seminaries ordinarily try to insure that their graduates learn to avoid that option, and I will admit that they are not always pleased with the results. As a liberal, if I identify some portion or theme of scripture as hopelessly disordered, I do not pretend to stand above scripture's traditioning process. I am instead playing a minor part in that very same process, which is the only way I know to be faithful to its most basic demands. I still find myself obliged to converse even with those portions of scripture I presently find most appalling. But just as I confess Jesus as the Christ because I finally cannot help myself, so do I also frequently find myself unable to keep from acknowledging that there is much in scripture that runs counter to that confession.

As a liberal I also have to acknowledge that scripture's traditioning process can be challenged by voices from other traditions that know little or nothing of the Christian witness— or have in some cases even arisen in outright opposition to it. It is true enough that sometimes these other voices can actually help me to recover parts of my own tradition that had previously escaped my attention, but I cannot accept their aid without welcoming their challenge, because the two usually go hand in hand. I have in mind here not just the varieties of secularism that have developed over the past three hundred years, but also the religious traditions of the East and Middle East, post-Christian spirituality here in the West, and of course Judaism, which refuses to let Christians— or secularists—get away with turning it into a museum piece.

Now the sharp differences among these traditions cannot be glossed over by some secondhand, Jungian type of syncretism, but to say that they do not have enough in common at least to challenge one another amounts to burying one's head

84

in the sand. Taking these voices seriously *does not* mean I have
to surrender my conviction that everybody needs to understand what God is doing for all of us in Jesus Christ, but
neither does that conviction mean that what I might still learn
from them is any less important. I may wind up being pulled
in several directions at once, but I do not think that is
anything new for Christians who know their own traditions—how else did we ever come up with the Trinity?

I suppose I should point out that so far I have been
describing liberal Christians as I think they ought to be,
which involves some fairly lofty ideals that nobody really
lives up to. One could go on all day in this vein, but this is
enough to say about liberalism to enable us to look at where
Scholer's position seems to stand in relation to it.

We seem to agree on a number of fundamental points.
We both seem to begin with a fundamental trust in an overall
traditioning process that involves multiple witnesses, including the witness that each of us finally has to bear whenever interpretations are attempted. We both seem to agree
that there is no point in this process that is not, in Scholer's
words, "thoroughly embedded in particular and conditioned
historical-cultural places or moments."[1] Neither of us, I hope,
could be confused with inerrantists or modernists. Of course
our positions do not coincide perfectly on these points, but I
detect very little tension between them.

I do, however, detect significant tensions over two further issues. Whether those tensions amount to outright
disagreement awaits further discussion.

First is the issue of how best to honor the plurality of
witnesses within the Bible itself. Like Scholer, and also like
Luke Johnson, I recognize that scholars in the past have been
too quick either to harmonize the witnesses by making them
say something they did not say or else to exclude those that
did not fit some sort of "canon within the canon." It is the
latter "canon within the canon" strategy that liberals have
advocated. Scholer and Johnson seem to suggest that we
would do better to let this diversity play itself out in the
churches' ongoing interpretive struggles. I agree at least up

to a point. This is precisely why I have found David Tracy's model of the working canon congenial: It is intended as a liberal alternative to the canon-within-the-canon approach. It suggests that there are many tensions among the biblical witnesses that are better left unresolved, because it is precisely among those tensions that we find the only kind of reconciliation there is to be had between God's life and ours. But I would go on to add that one can be faithful to this insight and still be obliged to conclude that some of that diversity finally amounts to a contradiction, and I do not know whether Scholer would agree with that or not. I cannot find a fruitful tension between testimonies to God's unconditional love and portrayals of God commanding acts of genocide. It seems immoral even to look for a fruitful tension there. And I am sure that Scholer would not call this a fruitful tension either, but then I wonder what he *would* call it, besides a contradiction.

The other issue, with which I will conclude, concerns how we are to conceive Jesus Christ's relationship to all these witnesses in a way that does justice to their actual diversity. How do we reconcile that diversity with Scholer's obviously Christocentric approach? I would claim to be Christocentric in some sense myself, but only in a way that neither excludes nor subordinates other, related but distinct, centers of loyalty and trust. Again, trinitarian thought in the early church seems, apart from its patriarchal imagery, to offer precedents for this latter kind of Christocentrism. It reminds us that God's unity does not exclude or subordinate *every* kind of plurality. Perhaps the same can be said for Scripture's elusive unity, and for the unity that continues to elude Christians arguing over biblical authority.

NOTE

[1] Evangelical Quarterly 60:1 (1988), p. 11.

4

The Authority of the New Testament in the Church: A Theological Reflection

Luke Johnson

My remarks are straightforwardly prescriptive rather than descriptive. I neither know nor have much interest in the range of scholarly opinions on this issue, which is not really, after all, a matter of scholarship. So this is an attempt at theological position-staking.

I have been assigned the "liberal" slot in this discussion, although on most issues having to do with interpretation I feel almost moss-backed with conservatism. On the issue of canon and church in particular I am positively rigid. But concerning the use of the Bible in the church my position can fairly be described as liberal in the sense that it presumes and encourages that liberty of the children of God given by the Spirit. The text that I would choose to adorn this reflection is precisely the one from 2 Corinthians 3:17: "Where the Spirit of the Lord is, there is freedom" (NRSV). Freedom is not to be equated with slovenliness or carelessness. Indeed, faith's freedom is the most rigorous of all asceticisms.

My position on biblical authority is liberal as well because it emphasizes the dialectical relationship between text and reader. But what texts? Some limitations of the subject are imperative. I will address myself primarily to the authority of the New Testament. I will touch only tangentially on the authority of Torah, asserting that, in the context of the church, all readings of Torah must pass at least implicitly through the prism of the New Testament.

Another limitation: I am considering only the question of the New Testament's authority as read text, leaving aside all the fascinating but distracting ways authority is ascribed to the book as sacred object. The Bible is treated as authority of some sort when we incense it, carry it in procession, open it with closed eyes and point to a passage, wave it in preaching, bow before it, cover it with jewels, swear by it in court. In the Christian religion, the Bible has undoubtedly had more authority in this talismanic way than as read text. Bell, Book, and Candle have seldom paused for solemn exegesis. But I must leave aside this too little explored aspect of religious phenomenology to address the authority of the text as read.

The meaning of the word *authority* is also problematic. The New Testament supplies a number of possible antecedents ranging from *dynamis*, with its nuance of impersonal power, to *exousia*, with its suggestion of freedom. Fuller remarks will come at the end of this essay, but it can be said at once that if we are speaking of the authority of a text as text, then we cannot mean something that simply inheres in the book as book; we must mean a quality that appears in the act of reading.

The most important preliminary consideration is a very specific framework and context for reading the New Testament. To establish that context as rapidly as possible, I will repeat a series of points I made at the end of my book, *The Writings of the New Testament: An Interpretation*, that I call "canonical theses."

Some Canonical Theses

1. The canon is the church's working bibliography. Whatever else is read and studied by individual Christians in private, these writings are used by the assembly as such for debating and defining its identity. These are, therefore, the public documents of the church. They are public in the sense that their first use is to be read aloud in worship. They are also public because they offer themselves to the entire community's debate and discernment.

2. The canon is more than the residuum of a historical process. It is a faith decision for the church to make in every age and place. The acceptance of these specific writings by a community—not by council but in liturgical use—is the most fundamental identity decision the church makes. The choice excludes contemporary writings that would make a similar claim for allegiance, and thereby asserts continuity with the community's past, and assumes responsibility for transmitting the same measure to the church in the future.

3. The canon and the church are, therefore, correlative concepts. The canon establishes discrete writings from the past as this community's scripture. Without a church there can be no canon; without canon there is no scripture in the fullest sense. As the church stands under the norm of scripture in every age, finding life and meaning in the reading of it, so do these writings find their realization as scripture by being so read by a community, age after age, as the measure of its life and meaning.

4. It is the nature of a canon to be closed. An unlimited canon is no measure, any more than a foot ruler can gain inches and still be a foot ruler. Because it is closed, the canon can perform the function of mediating a specific identity through successive ages of the church. Because the church today reads the same writings as were read by Polycarp and Augustine and Aquinas and Luther and Barth, it remains identifiably the same community, and on that basis can debate with those earlier readers their interpretations and realizations of that identity. Only a steady measure can provide such continuity. The discovery of a lost apostolic

letter would occasion excitement but could not be included in the canon, for it had never shaped the identity of the catholic church.

5. Because the canon is closed and exclusive, it can be catholic, that is, have universal and enduring pertinence. This is only an apparent paradox. A measure that can be altered by addition or subtraction at any time or place has no capacity to address every time and place.

6. What distinguishes the biblical scholar and theologian from the historian of ideas or student of literature is the effective recognition of the canon. For history and literature as such, the concept of canon is meaningless, except as a convenient categorization, or as the recognition that a certain group of writings achieved classical status at a certain time. These fall short of affirming the distinctive interrelationship between specific texts and a living community over an extended period of time essential to the notion of canon.

7. The ecclesial decision to regard these writings as scripture bears with it the recognition that they have a peculiar and powerful claim on the lives of individuals and above all on the community as a whole. The church asserts that it does not control these writings but that they in a very real sense control it, by providing the definitive frame for its self-understanding. Within the church, the critical questions posed to the texts by a reader are far less significant than the critical questions the texts pose to the reader.

8. Implicit in the recognition of the canonical writings as scripture is the acknowledgment that they not only speak in the voice of their human authors but also speak for an Other. The New Testament speaks prophetically to every age. Analytic to the concept of prophecy is the speaking of God's Word. These texts play a critical role in the process of God's revelation. Within their time-conditioned words and symbols, which come from many persons in the past, there speaks as well the singular Word of God, which endures through the ages. This conviction can be expressed by the statement that the texts are "divinely inspired," for to speak of the Word of God is to speak as well by implication of the work of God's

Spirit. Divine inspiration is one of the ways of expressing the unique authority Christians attribute to these writings. Explanations and interpretations of inspiration obviously vary widely, ranging from psychological theories that virtually equate it with literary inspiration, through metaphysical distinctions between primary and secondary causes, to the attribution of the whole creative process of composition within the social context of earliest Christianity to the real but subtle working of the Holy Spirit as part of the constitutive act of creating church.

9. Since the canon consists of a disparate collection of writings, with both the Old Testament and New Testament forming the Christian Bible, it resists reduction to any single unifying principle imposed from without as much as it lacks any explicit unifying principle within. If it excludes by its nature any "canon within the canon," it certainly also resists any conceptual mold that either relativizes or removes the texts themselves in all their hard particularity.

The resistance applies as well to any "New Testament theology." In all its forms, New Testament theology is simply another attempt to reduce the many to one by means of some abstract unifying principle, whether it is denominated salvation history or justification or liberation or *kerygma* or *regula fidei* or narrativity or existential decision. All such principles demand the selection of some texts as *a priori* more central and governing than others. All fit the writings themselves to frames of greater or lesser abstraction. The canon resists such attempts precisely because it is made up of multiple and irreducible writings that cannot without distortion be shaped into a static symbolic system.

On the other hand, the canon opens itself to the doing of theology in the church, which is another sort of enterprise altogether. In theology proper, the experience of God in contemporary human lives and events is articulated and brought into a faithful dialogue with all the writings of the Old and New Testaments, not in an attempt to fix their meaning but in a living conversation that ranges freely and leads to surprising results.

10. Since the canon consists of the public documents of a community that have as their natural context proclamation in the liturgical assembly, the church requires a hermeneutic appropriate to the nature of the canon. Such a hermeneutic would not be concerned primarily with the reading of the text by individuals for their pleasure or transformation. This sort of reading has had all sorts of interpretive models from allegory through existential interpretation to reader-response. None of these need be rejected. Freedom and fantasy open the minds and hearts of people. But such models of interpretation scarcely reach the neighbor, and do not provide a way of reading the texts in their primary function, which is to mediate the identity of the church as church.

What is needed is a properly *ecclesial hermeneutic,* one that places the writings in their canonical context and that involves the entire faith community in the interpretive process. For such a hermeneutic to work, there must be the active discernment of the work of God in the lives of contemporary believers, raised to the level of a narrative of faith; there must be, at the same time, the active discernment of the canonical texts in the light of these contemporary experiences and narratives. This process of discernment must occur in a public context that enables discussion, debate, disagreement, and decision. In this creative if tension-filled context, the canonical witnesses can again shape the identity of the Christian community.

A Midrashic Model for an Ecclesial Hermeneutic

The formation of an ecclesial hermeneutic should follow the process by which the writings of the New Testament themselves came into existence and allow the dialectic of experience and interpretation to come alive again. The New Testament writings came into being in the first place by means of a process best termed midrashic. The tensions between sacred texts and powerful religious experiences forced new understandings and eventually a restructured symbolic world. It is the fundamental conviction of faith that such powerful religious experiences continue to occur in our world. People continue to encounter the living God in however dark and oblique ways.

But as the church today seeks to deal with the tensions between text and experience, it is not only the symbolic world of Torah that requires negotiation but also the texts of the New Testament itself; this symbolic world too must be re-shaped and renewed by the continuing experience of the Spirit in and outside the church, and come to new clarity in the interpretive context of the community.

Just as midrash is a category that enables us to under-stand the process of the text's creation, so is it a category that enables us to move in the direction of a properly ecclesial hermeneutic. The Christian church can again learn some-thing from Judaism and regard the New Testament canon as analogous to the Talmud.

As the Talmud was a crystallization of a long history of interpretation of Torah mediated by new experiences, which became authoritative for the Jewish tradition not as the replacement of Torah but as the inescapable prism through which Torah would be read and understood, so can the New Testament writings be regarded as crystallizations of reflec-tion on Torah in the light of the experience of Jesus the crucified Messiah and risen Lord. The New Testament writings remain authoritative and normative for the Chris-tian tradition not as the replacement of Torah but as the indispensable prism through which Torah is to be read and understood.

There is, of course, this important difference: In the Talmud there are not separate writings but a diversity of voices, whereas in the New Testament there is diversity both of voice and of literary form. But there is also this even more critical similarity: In the study of Talmud, one never listens to only one voice or authority. One never follows the views of Rabbi Judah through every tractate or of Rabbi Eliezer on every topic. Nor does the study of Talmud yield a single abstractable answer that need not be reinterpreted in the light of changing circumstances. Indeed, the whole point of midrash is to hear the various voices in all their conflicts and disagreements, for it is precisely in those elements of plurality and even disharmony that the texts open themselves to new meaning, so that they are allowed to speak to the disharmonies and disjunctions of contemporary life.

In just such a fashion, Christians should learn to read the canon of the New Testament, not in the search for an essential core or purified canon within the canon, not within the frame of a single abstract principle, but in a living conversation with all the writings in their diversity and divergence.

Meanings of Authority

Within the context of church and canon, these three aspects of authority can be distinguished.

1. *The New Testament as Author.*

Of first importance for the Christian community is the New Testament's ability to *author*, that is to create a certain identity in its readers, to bring a Christian community into existence or renew it. Whether read in the assembly or by lonely individuals in motel rooms and prison cells, the writings can shape a new and distinctive consciousness, empower capacities that were previously not there. The New Testament has transformative power. There is nothing magical or even specifically theological in this: The reading of Shakespeare after all has created poets and lovers of poetry. What is specifically theological is the church's conviction that this authoring power of the scripture is activated by the Holy Spirit. All texts can transform, but these texts transform according to the mind of Christ.

It is in this identity function that the New Testament has the greatest degree of unanimity within the variety of its literary forms and distinctive authorial perspectives. The writings converge on the matter of identity: the meaning of life before God in light of a crucified and raised Messiah whose Spirit enlivens a character expressed by faith, hope, and love, and which dispositions in turn are enacted by the messianic pattern of life for others that govern both individual consciousness and the dynamics of interaction in the community. These are not the special insights of Paul or

James or John, but ground all the writings at the deep level of implicit agreement that enabled a *regula fidei* to be constructed in the first place. Here is where the New Testament is most reliable and trustworthy, most deserving of the designation *inerrant*, for it is in this realm of what Roman Catholicism in another connection calls "faith and morals" that we touch on the real subject matter of the New Testament writings.

Because now this aspect and now that aspect of authentic Christian identity function is found in the respective writings, they must all be read for that identity to be properly formed. A Christian consciousness based solely on the gospel of John would surely be distorted in the direction of exclusivism and sectarianism without the saving irony of the gospel of Mark. A Christian identity based solely on Paul as purveyor of *sola fide* would be distorted in the direction of pietism without the challenge to practical morality posed by the Letter of James.

This identity function is fulfilled best and most reliably when the documents are read in liturgy, where the ritual of the community and the critical reflection of preaching alike can work as co-authors of identity. The power of these texts to form identity is certainly as powerful—perhaps even more so because undiluted—in the case of private reading, but it is also more dangerous because it is unconditioned by community debate and discernment. What Paul said of prophecy in the assembly should apply as well to the private reading of scripture: "Let all discern" (1 Cor. 14:29).

2. *The New Testament as Authorizer.*

The New Testament canon also provides authorization for its own interpretation. Its identity function moved toward definition and integrity—this pattern of life is authentically Christian, that one is not—but its authorizing function moves toward freedom, the empowerment of its readers.

By "authority" here I mean what the Latin term *auctoritas* includes as examples and warrants. The New Testament provides its readers with examples of ways in which authoritative texts can freely be reread in light of new experience and the working of the Spirit—without thereby ceasing to be normative. The most obvious example is the re-reading of Torah in the light of the crucified Messiah. The New Testament writers do not seem to think the authority of Torah makes it immune from interpretation, even of the boldest sort. Paul's "history of salvation" in Romans 9-11 appears nowhere in Torah itself and is legitimated only by his conviction that Messiah is the *telos* of Torah. On the same basis, Paul denies the authority of Torah as commandment while upholding its authority as narrative in Galatians 3-4. The hermeneutical options of midrash, typology, and allegory so important for the history of Christian interpretation are all given by the New Testament itself.

Such freedom of interpretation is applied not only to Torah, but also to the story of Jesus. How else can we account for the development of the synoptic tradition, in which first the oral tradition is worked into a narrative by Mark, and then re-interpreted in quite divergent ways by Matthew and Luke without the suppression of the earlier version? Or how account for the idiosyncratic reworking of the gospel tradition by John accepted side by side in the canon with those other three? As historians we observe the *exousia* exercised by the first Christian writers but we hesitate—far more than did our ancestors Clement and Origen!—to appropriate it ourselves.

The New Testament also provides *exempla* that authorize certain hermeneutical activities in the church, such as the process of reaching decision. In my small book, *Decision Making in the Church*, I have analyzed the narrative account in Acts 10-15 about the decision to grant Gentiles full status in the church, not simply as a historical record but as a scriptural warrant for the church in our own age reaching decisions in the same fashion: by hearing the narratives of faith based in the experiences of contemporary believers and allowing debate and discernment of those narratives lead to new understandings of scripture itself. For Acts, it was a new understanding of the prophet Amos; for Christians today, even of Acts itself.

3. The New Testament as a Collection of Auctoritates.

A third meaning of authority applies to the thematic level of the New Testament writings, where the diversity of literary forms and divergence of opinions is most obvious. On any number of issues it is simply impossible to reconcile what New Testament writers have to say on the same subject. The answer to the question, "What does the New Testament have to say about X?" is often, "It depends on what you have read last." If we ask, for example, "What is the Christian attitude toward the State?" we must consider at least the chasm between Romans and 1 Peter on one side, and Revelation on the other. If we ask, "What is the proper Christian attitude toward the world?" we would have an even more complex range of views, running from the irenicism of 1 Peter through the intricate "as though not" of Paul to the radical sectarianism of the Johannine letters.

We would meet the same divergence on other questions, down to and including the best way to describe Jesus, an obvious factor in the internecine battles over christological definitions for some six centuries. If we turn to such practical matters as when and how to baptize or celebrate the Lord's Supper or organize a community, the sad history of Christianity illustrates just how obviously it is possible to prove anything on the basis of the New Testament, so long as a certain judicious selectivity and suppression of evidence is carried out.

What do we make then of this thematic jumble? In the first place, we exercise common sense and make a healthy distinction. If the New Testament writings agree so powerfully on the shape of Christian identity but differ so much on the specifics of its articulation in the world, this might mean two things: The first is that identity is more important than ritual consistency; the second is that the New Testament actually legitimizes a healthy pluralism of practice within the same basic identity.

Within that diversity, in turn, we are allowed to exercise the *exousia* given by the New Testament itself with regard to Torah. We resist the urge to make only one such *auctoritas* (or

98

opinion) normative to the exclusion of others. We avoid the temptation to an easy or false harmonization. Rather, as with the opinions in Talmud, we enter into a conversation with these diverse views and opinions expressed by the New Testament, finding in their areas of overlap as well as in their points of divergence guidance for our own decisions.

But in the end, none of the options may represent our practice as individuals or as community. What then? If we do not *do* exactly what these statements direct, how can we call them an authority? Because we take them into account. Every Christian community, as every Christian, stands to some degree or other in disagreement with some part of the New Testament. Anyone who claims otherwise is simply lying. The issue of biblical authority therefore is not whether it gives a consistent blueprint for every aspect of our lives, or that our lives conform exactly to that blueprint. Given the diversity within the canon, any such claim would be specious. The issue of authority is whether the texts are taken seriously as normative, even when— as often—they diverge or even disagree.

Taking the texts seriously means that in our ecclesial—as well as personal—decisions we are willing to take our stand over against as well as under the text. Do we allow divorce in our community despite Jesus' clear condemnation of divorce? Then we do not live in accord with this text. To be faithful to the scripture, we cannot suppress its reading; we must be able to say *why* we do not live in accord with its clear directive. This means that we must find *authorization* for our position somewhere else in these writings. Sometimes we will be given an option by the divergence given by another text, or by the *exousia* of reinterpretation in the light of new experiences of God's work in human lives and events. The limit to such *exousia*, in turn, will be set by the integrity of the individual and community identity as measured by the messianic pattern authored by these same writings.

These observations apply to the other positions we adopt concerning such matters as women ministers or the equality of women in the household or to our taking of oaths or to our equation of Christianity with mental and physical well-being and material comfort and the American way of life. There is no room for sloppiness and shoddiness in these matters. It is not scholarship that demands precision as well as passion in the reading of the New Testament. As John Updike said in another context, "precision is a function of attention and attention is a function of concern."[1] If we are not precise in these things, then we do not care. And carelessness is as good a candidate as any for the sin against the Spirit.

Conclusion

Such, I submit, are the complex ways in which "the authority of the New Testament for the church" is to be understood. My analysis separates levels of normativity, not on the basis of antiquity or authorship, but on the basis of functions. Identity is the presupposition for freedom—freedom more importantly than conformity. When I have shared these ideas before, my listeners express fear at the risks involved. This makes me wonder whether we take seriously enough the truth that existence itself leaves us no other authentic option, when we confess that we are in the hands of a living God. The greatest risk is to refuse listening, to close ourselves institutionally or ideologically to the God who seeks to carve a space for His freedom in our hearts.

But fear is in any case unnecessary. The freedom to read in the way I have suggested is conditioned by a strong view of church and canon. It presupposes that the texts are read as a church makes decisions, and that discernment is allowed to take place. In all honesty, I am not sanguine about the possibilities for these premises existing in real-life communities calling themselves Christian. On the evidence it is not the texts as read that are taken seriously, but the book as object, as power source, as icon, as talisman. Is it only the scholar in me that finds this a cause for sad contemplation?

NOTE

[1]John Updike, *Picked-up Pieces* (New York: Alfred A. Knopf, 1975), p. 248.

A Conservative Response

John O. Hosler

Though I consider myself an evangelical conservative, I may be representing only a few of those who similarly classify themselves. Like Dr. Johnson, I do not have a talismanic view of biblical authority. However, I also do not have a talismanic view of my own heart, conscience, intuition, nor of the consensus of the church as a community.

. In addition to the written Torah, the Pharisees and rabbis recognized an oral Torah that comprised specific applications of the general principles of the written Torah. In Christ's day the oral traditions went beyond application to the establishment of an extra-textual orthodoxy that was assigned equal authority with the scriptures. This practice literally resulted in the cancellation of the written Word of God (Matt. 15:2; Mark 7:9, 13; Col. 2:8). I believe that this same error is being committed in our own time in the name of "The Living Logos."

101

Some contemporary theologians attribute to themselves or to the community of believers the same authority as that possessed by the apostles. I prefer to interpret the words *dynamis* and *exousia* within their contextual usage and not merely by their lexical definitions. In so doing, I would note that the power and authority of the sacred text is of a different domain and thus not the same as the *exousia* of government (cf. Luke 19:17; Acts 9:14: the Sanhedrin; Luke 20:20: Pilate). It is also different from the God-given power of self-determination in the believer (Acts 5:4); the satanic power of kings (Rev. 17:12), and "the powers that be" (Luke 12:11; Rom. 13:1). It is not the same as the sphere of the state's dominion (Luke 23:7), the domain of spirits (Eph. 2:3), nor of the spiritual powers (1 Cor. 15:24; Eph. 1:21; Col. 1:16; 1 Peter 3:22).

First, God possesses *exousia* as the source of all power and legality (Luke 12:5; Acts 1:7; Jude 25; Rom. 9:21). Secondly, all natural forces derive their *exousia* from God (Rev. 6:8; 9:3, 10, 19; 16:9; 18:1). Thirdly, God's will also encompasses Satan's sphere of dominion (Acts 26:18; Col. 1:13). Fourthly, God's *exousia* and *dynamis* are fully possessed by Jesus Christ in His deity (Matt. 28:18; Rev. 12:10).

The church has a power of self-determination as is clearly seen in Acts 15. But this is a freedom to embrace as well as to reject error. When Christ prophesied the immediate entering in of false prophets He was declaring that God would not forcibly prohibit error in the church (Matt. 7:15, 22, 23). It was the church's task to defend itself from error (Jude 3). But by what rule? If there was not a rule distinct from the body of saints that would serve as an effective tool, then either the will of the saints would become the rule or else the will of the ecclesiastical hierarchy would become the authoritative canon law for the church. In such a case we would have a repetition of the problem of the Pharisees and scribes negating the *exousia* of the sacred writings (Matt. 15:6, 9).

My position is that the Bible is the rule or canon for the church. Because I am not by my Adamic nature a humble man, I must take steps to protect myself from my own pride.

Therefore, I attempt to require that none of my Christian doctrines will have originated with myself or my denomination. They must have originated with Christ and have been delivered to the church via the original apostles and through the scriptures. Although the redeemed body of Christ is universal, doctrines that originated from that body are not catholic. The only catholic doctrines are those delivered to that body by the apostles.

Thus, the doctrinal *exousia* chain of command begins with the entire Trinity and is delivered to the church through the apostles. Even before the scriptures were complete, the "apostolic tradition" had become a closed system of doctrine (Jude 3; 2 Thess. 3:6; Rom. 16:17; Gal. 1:6-9). Dr. Johnson had told us that it is the nature of a canon to be closed. This is certainly true.

The early church sought to protect itself from error with a closed system of pre-canon orthodoxy called the "apostolic tradition." Before this norm reached a fixity of expression it was not possible for a definite canon to come into existence. The actual term "canon" was not in use until the fourth century. So, instead of "canon" I will use the word "authority." The recognition of doctrinal authority was observed during the second-century anti-gnostic debates. The primary criterion in such debates was the usage of a closed system of doctrine among groups known to have held the traditional "faith of the apostles."

In John 14:26, Christ proclaimed to the apostles that the Holy Ghost would "teach you all things and will remind you of everything I have said to you."[1] In John 16:13 Christ said that the Spirit of Truth would guide the apostles into "all truth." This was a promise of total accuracy based upon total recall of what was spoken by Christ. I understand that neither myself nor the community of believers possesses such an authority. We only have the information that was delivered to us through the apostles. Believers are "members of God's household, built on the foundation of the apostles and prophets, with Christ Jesus himself as the chief cornerstone" (Eph. 2:19-21).

Clement, the third bishop of the congregation at Rome, who was conversant with the apostles, refers to a pre-canon closed system of orthodoxy in his First Epistle to the Corinthians:

(Chap. XLII) The apostles have preached the Gospel to us from the Lord Jesus Christ; Jesus Christ has done so from God. Christ therefore was sent forth by God, and the apostles by Christ. Both these appointments, then, were made in an orderly way, according to the will of God. Having therefore received their orders, and being fully assured by the resurrection of our Lord Jesus Christ, and established in the word of God, with full assurance of the Holy Ghost, they went forth proclaiming that the kingdom of God was at hand.[2]

Ignatius of the church of Antioch in Syria is remembered as a co-disciple with Polycarp of the apostle John. He also refers to a pre-canon orthodoxy in his Epistle to the Magnesians:

(Chap. XIII) Study, therefore to be established in the doctrines of the Lord and of the apostles, so that all things, whatsoever ye do, may prosper, both in the flesh and spirit, in faith and love.

Thus, I believe that true catholic unity must be based on a closed system of apostolic doctrine. In his Epistle to the Romans, Ignatius distinguishes between his authority as a bishop and the authority of the apostles: (Chap. IV) "I do not, as Peter and Paul, issue commandments unto you. They were apostles of Jesus Christ, but I am the very least [of believers]."

Irenaeus states the case for us in the preface of this third book, Against Heresies, where he points out that his truth is qualified in that it did not originate with himself:

But in this, the third book, I shall adduce proofs from the Scriptures, so that I may come behind in nothing of what thou hast enjoined; yea, that over and above what thou receive, thou mayest receive from me the means of combating and vanquishing those who, in whatever manner, are propagating falsehood. For the love of God, being rich and ungrudging, confers upon the suppliant more than he can ask from it. Call to mind, then, the things which I have stated in the two preceding books, and, taking these in connection with them, thou shalt have from me a very copious refutation of all the heretics; and faithfully and strenuously shalt thou resist them in defence of the only true and life-giving faith, which the Church has received from the apostles and imparted to her sons. For the Lord of all gave to His apostles the power of the Gospel, through whom also we have known the truth, that is, the doctrine of the Son of God; to whom also did the Lord declare: "He that heareth you, heareth Me; and he that despiseth you, despiseth me, and Him that sent Me."

Again in Chapter I Irenaeus states that:

We have learned from none others the plan of our salvation, than from those through whom the Gospel has come down to us, which they did at one time proclaim in public, and, at a later period, by the will of God, handed down to us in the Scriptures, to be the ground and pillar of our faith.

Irenaeus describes heretics as those who claimed to have received new truth from God to be added to the apostolic tradition and demonstrates the task of the presbyters as that of keeping the system closed:

(Chap. II) But, again, when we refer them to that tradition which originates from the apostles [and] which is preserved by means of the successions of presbyters in the Churches, they object to tradition, saying that they themselves are wiser not merely than the presbyters, but even than the apostles, because they have discovered the unadulterated truth.

Irenaeus tells us that it is this closed system that makes Christian doctrine public and therefore catholic:

> (Chap. III) It is within the power of all, therefore, in every Church, who may wish to see the truth, to contemplate clearly the tradition of the apostles manifested throughout the whole world; and we are in a position to reckon up those who were by the apostles instituted bishops in the Churches, and [to demonstrate] the succession of these men to our own times; those who neither taught nor knew of anything like what these [heretics] rave about. For if the apostles had known hidden mysteries, which they were in the habit of imparting to "the perfect" apart and privily from the rest, they would have delivered them especially to those to whom they were also committing the Churches themselves.

He further illustrates this point by listing in succession the first twelve bishops of the Church at Rome in relation to their obligation to keep the system closed.

> (Chap. III) In this order, and by this succession, the ecclesiastical tradition from the apostles, and the preaching of the truth, have come down to us. And this is most abundant proof that there is one and the same vivifying faith, which has been preserved in the Church from the apostles until now, and handed down in truth.

Irenaeus continues by using Polycarp to illustrate the sole authority of the apostolic tradition.

> (Chap. III) But Polycarp also was not only instructed by apostles, and conversed with many who had seen Christ, but was also, by apostles in Asia, appointed bishop of the Church in Smyrna, whom I also saw in my early youth. . . and, when a very old man, gloriously and most nobly suffering martyrdom, departed this life, having always taught the things which he had learned from the apostles, and which the Church

has handed down and which alone are true. To these things all the Asiatic Churches testify, as do also those men who have succeeded Polycarp down to the present time....He it was who, coming to Rome in the time of Anicetus caused many to turn away from the aforesaid heretics to the Church of God, proclaiming that he had received this one and sole truth from the apostles.

This is why Irenaeus considers it unnecessary to seek for extra-apostolic information regarding the will of God.

(Chap. IV) Since therefore we have such proofs, it is not necessary to seek the truth among others which it is easy to obtain from the Church; since the apostles, like a rich man [depositing his money] in a bank, lodged in her hands most copiously all things pertaining to the truth.

This same idea of the sole authority of the apostolic tradition is equivalent to my belief in the sole authority of the scriptures for faith and doctrine. Irenaeus thus makes the conclusion:

(Chap. V) Since, therefore, the tradition from the apostles does thus exist in the Church, and is permanent among us, let us revert to the scriptural proof furnished by those apostles who did also write the Gospel, in which they recorded the doctrine regarding God, pointing out that our Lord Jesus Christ is the truth, and that no lie is in him.

The use of "the *kerygma*" as an overall term to denote the substance of the message of the New Testament and a skeleton framework underlying it is well founded. Paul's gospel was the same as the preaching of Jesus (Rom. 16:25) and any departure from it was to be avoided (Rom. 16:17; 2 Thess. 3:6; Acts 20:25-31). Thus, the true *kerygma* was committed to the church originally through the preaching of the apostles (Titus 1:3; 2 Tim. 4:17).

It is my position therefore that there is not a divine extrabiblical *kerygma* to be recognized by the church today. If there is, I know that I will never have the inerrant ability to distinguish it from the claims of false apostles (2 Cor. 11:13). My only hope of getting close to the truth is the sole authority of the Bible. I have no chance in the contemporary game of preacher roulette wherein one gambles his soul on a guess as to which "prophet" is really speaking the oracles of God. The New Testament church has an *exousia* that is a freedom for the community. This is not a freedom to correct the scriptures with spiritual authority in the name of the "Living Logos." When the apostle Paul spoke by "concession" or "permission" (*suggnome*), he was only offering personal advice and made it clear that this was not a commandment from God (1 Cor. 7:6). Though Timothy and Irenaeus were indwelt by the "Living Logos," they received no new doctrines that were not already handed down from the apostles: "And the things you have heard me say in the presence of many witnesses entrust to reliable men who will also be qualified to teach others" (2 Tim. 2:2). The Christian community is free to enter into error but not authorized to pontificate that the error is a revelational mandate from Christ. When the Christian community rejected the heliocentric view of the solar system it proved to the world that the canon for the church was not the consensus of the community nor of the hierarchs. The community's freedom is from the curse of the law (Rom. 6:14) and from the theological commandments of men (Col. 2:20-22), but not a freedom and authority to issue new commandments (1 Tim. 4:1-4). Thus, community *exousia* is not intrinsic divine autonomy from the authority of scripture. Christian gnosticism seems to have developed a freedom along the lines of the extremists at Corinth (1 Cor. 5:1 ff.). In the apocryphal Acts, as is often the case today, *exousia* was a mystically extorted power deployed for one's own ends.

Although God reveals Himself in nature (Rom. 1:20) and in the conscience of man (Rom. 1:18, 19), these revelations contain no doctrines that are not already declared in scripture (Rom. 2:14). I am often charged with limiting God to the content of the scriptures and thus putting Him in a box. I know that God is infinite and therefore cannot be limited. However, I would be attempting to limit God if I proclaimed that He is incapable of placing scriptural boundaries on what He will allow us to know about His will for mankind. I am a limited agnostic like the apostle Paul. I believe that extrabiblical information about the will of God is past finding out (Rom. 11:33; James 4:13-16). It is not that the infinite God is limited to this Book. The limitation is that I am small and finite and therefore my understanding is limited to the canon.

I also believe that the body of Christ has a mission and that the scriptures contain all the doctrinal furnishings to perform every work in that objective (2 Tim. 3:16, 17). I have never said that God cannot reveal new truth beyond the scriptures. However, I would be limiting God if I insisted that He must reveal extrabiblical truth to me whether He desires to do so or not. I would be limiting God to say that He cannot close the canon.

Laying aside the issue of canonical authority there arises the question of interpretation. I require of myself not to have a talismanic view of my own feelings nor of the consensus of the Christian community. In order for the canon to be a public measuring rod it must self-contain the key to its own interpretation. I require that my method of interpretation, as well as the revelation I use, be objectively outside myself. I believe that a correct guess regarding biblical meaning is absolutely improbable. Is it not rational to conclude that the writers had a particular meaning in mind for each text? Is it not also reasonable to conclude that they intended for that meaning to be ascertained? I have concluded that I will live long enough to uncover only a portion of all the answers to Bible questions. However, this does not mean that the answers are not there. An objective historical-grammatical analysis of a text will give me more truth than any alternative I know. If I cannot find the hermeneutical key to the correct interpretation of a text, I will refuse to guess or look inside myself for a mystical key. What a text means must be contained within the text itself and within the coherent context of the entire canon. Otherwise, my correct understanding would require a further revelation, which some contemporary scholars refer to as "illumination." On the contrary, the true gospel does not need lighting, it is light (2 Cor. 4:4). Furthermore, the Word of God does not need to be lit, it is the illumination of God when properly read and understood (Ps. 119:105). My recommendation to each member of the Christian community is to read and hear the scriptures with heed, caution, and discretion, attempting to recognize when the preacher or the community is departing from textual authority.

My hermeneutical approach to a text is therefore no dialectic. I do not bring my objections to a text as an antithesis and work toward a compromise position between it and myself. There is a vast difference between assigning a new meaning to a text and deriving a further interpretation from it. If change or progression occurs in my understanding, it must be the text that changes me and not myself who changes the text.

When contradictions seem apparent in the Bible, as in the case of Paul's faith without works and James' faith plus works, I must have confidence that God's true Word cannot be self-contradictory and that two contradictory positions cannot simultaneously be true. I know that I am in no position to choose which of the two positions are of God. If the Bible is infallible and coherent in matters of faith and doctrine, then there is something that I am missing. Paul said we are "justified by faith apart from observing the law" (Rom. 3:28) while James proclaimed that we are justified by works and "not by faith alone" (James 2:24). Paul described faith without works as very much alive (Rom. 4:5) while James affirmed that the same faith without works is "dead" (James 2:17). Paul declared that Abraham was not justified by works in the sight of God (Rom. 4:2) while James proposes that Abraham was justified by works (James 2:21).

What am I missing? The key to Romans chapter four is "but not before God" (4:2) while the key to James' chapter two is "Show me your faith without deeds, and I will show you my faith by what I do" (James 2:18). Paul is speaking of justification in the sight of God while James is addressing justification in the sight of man—"Show me...and I will show you." God can see my faith when I am sitting silently on a bench and eating an apple. You can recognize me as a Christian only by my testimony and my deeds. There is no contradiction between these texts.

In my view, the inner witness of the "Living Logos" and the outer witness of the scriptures are the same in content. "Anyone who believes in the Son of God has this testimony in his heart. Anyone who does not believe God has made him out to be a liar, because he has not believed the testimony God has given about his Son. And this is the testimony: God has given us eternal life" (1 John 5:10, 11). "I write these things to you who believe in the name of the Son of God so that you may know that you have eternal life" (1 John 5:13). The problem is this: If the Bible is not the sole authority for faith and doctrine, my only alternative is to find absolute information about God's will from another source. Who will be the first to arise and proclaim that the "Living Logos" has chosen to reveal that information through him or through his denomination?

NOTES

[1] All scriptural quotations in this essay are from the New International Version of the Bible.

[2] All quotations from the Apostolic Fathers are from The *Ante-Nicene Fathers*, ed. Rev. Alexander Roberts, D.D., and James Donaldson, LL.D., (Grand Rapids: Eerdmans, 1977).

A Moderate Response

George Tooze

We long for a sense of self disclosure from God. We long for a sense of (as well as a source of) authority upon which to base the life journey, the faith journey, to which we all are called. How are we to make our decisions and our commitments? Where are we to find this authority?

We seek for anchors and for certainty. We seek for a highway well marked along which we can move toward our destination, but we learn that the road we seek is but yet a path, and the path winds obtusely through the forest and thickets of confusion, ambivalence, and subjectivity. We thought we faced a simple task, but now we find that it is far more complex than we first imagined, and the task is perhaps even incapable of objectivity.

Dr. Johnson, along with the other writers, has attempted to give us some signposts for the journey. Dealing with his in particular, there are some that, in my opinion, are sharp and in focus and as I see them I applaud his sense of direction and the perceptiveness that he brings to the journey. There are however, other signs that he posts that I look at and I say, "I wish that they had just a bit more definition; I wish that they were just a bit more explicit." And, of course, there are a few signs that he places alongside the highway of our journey that I stand before and say to myself, "I don't know! I suspect if I go down there I'm going to end up someplace I really don't want to be!

I put the signposts in the categories: "I wish!" "I applaud!" "I wonder!"

I Wish

There are two signposts here. The first deals with the Bible as symbol. He touches on this and piques my interest, but then he quickly moves on. I think he dismisses the possibility of the Bible as symbol. And yet, might there not be a positive word to be said? I'd like to explore this area, for to me the Bible as symbol has some possibilities, a lot of meaning, and, I suspect, a lot of authority. It brings that authority inherent within it, for like the steeple of a church that points a finger to the heavens, so does the Bible as a symbol bring an authoritative Word from the God whom it represents to a number of places: to the sickroom of a patient, to a sanctuary as it sits upon an altar, to mention but two.

Then, secondly, I wish that he had incorporated the whole Bible in his presentation, not just the Torah and the New Testament. As I try to understand what he means by the New Testament as Midrash, as a window through which I am to view the Torah, as a window through which I am to view the Christ event, I wonder if or how the window applies to the writings, to the historical books, and to the prophets. Are they not of importance? How are we to view them? How are we to interpret the view that while we do understand the old through the new, the new may be shaped and formed by the old? There is no suggestion as to how that possibility fits into the equation. Are we, for example, to eliminate the image of the suffering servant of Second Isaiah from how we view the cross and the act of Jesus upon the cross? Are we to eliminate some of the themes of social justice from Amos, Isaiah, and Jeremiah and not see there a foundation for God's concern for the poor and dispossessed that we find expressed, for example, in the Magnificat of Mary, or in the teaching of Jesus? Is it possible that the Torah or the prophets or the writings are Midrashim for other portions of the scripture? Just where do we plant our feet to get the proper view or perspective?

I wish that we could have had a view of the whole, and not just a part, for the questions that remain seem imperative.

I Applaud

I applaud Johnson's emphasis that the biblical document is central to worship. Far too often it becomes merely a text for the preacher, a platform from which to be launched into a thousand different directions. Our worship must allow the texts to be central and it must allow the texts to bring that word from God to us that we so desperately need for the living of our lives.

I applaud his sense of continuity within the text. I wanted to sing with a great joy when I was reminded that the text I read is the same one that shaped Augustine and Calvin and Judson, and all of the history of thought and action within the church. I applaud the witness that the texts speak the Word of the "Other," that they convey a self-disclosure of the eternal, and that our God whom we believe we know in a personal sense can use the text as a tool to do work on and in the lives of individuals. I applaud that power that he gives the text to move us, even to transform us.

I applaud his resistance to most forms of theology. I know its necessity; I know that it is important to try to see a whole picture. Nevertheless, I am suspicious of it and always have been. I dislike compartments because they seem so inflexible and certainly some of the compartments that have been created have disrupted if not sought to divide and/or destroy the church. I applaud his idea of theology as dynamic, living, and continuous conversation that brings the text to real life.

I applaud his emphasis on dialogue, on the struggle that we must have with the context and the meaning within the context. We must get away from a rote interpretation based on a dictation of an individual, a study group, a church, a denomination. I would rather lose a person from the membership of my church because I do not preach easy or authoritative answers from my pulpit than give a single-sided view and insist that there are no other possibilities of interpretation. They need to explore these matters for themselves and come with the help of the Spirit to their own conclusions.

I Wonder
In the end, however, I do not have a clear sense of exactly where Johnson ultimately places his sense of authority. That may be due to my natural sense of confusion, or it may be due to some expressed ambivalence on his part. I long for authority to be in the text, inherent there because of the self-disclosure of God, having power because of that to work in individual lives. Johnson seems, in places, to agree. This was especially true as he spoke of the ability of the scripture to author.

In other places, however, he seems to diffuse that quality and to end up somewhere else. He says that authority is "a quality that appears in the act of reading" (p. 88). He suggests, for example, that there is authority in the process of inter-pretation and uses the example of the Midrash as a window. Beyond that he seems to suggest that there is authority in the interpretations of the church and the conclusions of its history and experience. But if it is in the *process* that authority is found, then I am concerned for its subjectivity, for process is subjective and really can move in any direction the winds will take it. This, indeed, is one of the scandals of the church.

If, on the other hand, authority is in the church, I am concerned for its fragility and frailty, for we are so divided and fractious. The church cannot even decide upon a canon; how can it decide upon a text and the meaning of that text?

The text has to exist independently of the interpretative judgment of the community, independently of any singular kind of process. Do we need any more than the Reformation model of the individual along with the text and the Holy Spirit? Do we need any more than the idea or the ideal of the priesthood of the individual believers who have, by the grace of God, a mind, a conscience, and a responsibility to be the arbitrator of how the authority of text is to speak to them and shape the form and course of their lives?

I wonder about his attempt to mesh authority and the scandal of our diversity. There is something in me that wants to hope that the body of Christ can be one, that the texts speak more clearly and with more unanimity than we would like to believe at times. I wonder if he doesn't leave us too divisive and at ease with that?

I am not sure that he really is a liberal in the sense that I understand it. He does give considerable authority to the text itself and my fantasy is that a liberal (the real thing!) would not. I remember a conversation I had with a preacher friend. He is a liberal and Johnson seems to be in a different place than he. Our conversation took place the day after Easter and he was commenting that his sermon had not been particularly well received the day before. I asked him what he had proclaimed to the congregation and he replied that he had told them that the resurrection had not really happened. To my "Oh?" he said, "I told them that the two on the road to Emmaus began talking to each other and as they talked and remembered, the memory seemed so real to them that Jesus really seemed to be there in their midst in person. They were so moved that they went out and told the story that Jesus was still alive and at work in the world, and this was an infection that spread to the other disciples as they were brought from their despair by the power of the memory of Jesus and all that was shared."

At the time it seemed to me that my friend's church was telling him that they wanted a sense of assurance and power that could speak to the meaning and problems of life. They did not seem to want an intellectual exercise that explained something away. They wanted a word of hope and of faith that would give them the courage to meet the needs of each day; they wanted that word based on something that was an authoritative disclosure of their God. His interpretation had removed that authoritative hope from them.

As did they, I too long for a word from God, a personal word, a word to guide me, a word to give me hope, a word to define my life, a word that I might be willing to die for if not to live for.

Out of this, on a practical basis at the very least, I need to assume the Spirit of God inherent in a context (that context being the scripture) and I have to assume that under the guidance of the Holy Spirit that word has authority to shape and mold my life. I want the text to have an authority within itself, an authority as the self-disclosure of my God. I want the authority to be there not because I put it there—not because of what I get out of it, not because of how it moves me, not because the church decides it to be something. I want it there because of what it is within itself, the word of a living God. I am willing to struggle with its meaning. I am willing to study it to whatever depth is needed. I am willing to dialogue with the text and with the community. But I need something with which to start, some place that says "I Am that I Am!" that conveys such authority within itself.

5

The Future of Biblical Authority: Implications for Public Policy Issues

Edgar A. Towne

There is a facile way to state the thesis of this paper, though once it is stated its underlying complexity will be apparent: The future of biblical authority is secure. What is not so secure are our faithfulness to God within this authority and our constitutional freedoms under law. The dialectical complexity of the situation can be shown by juxtaposing discipleship and citizenship, terms taken from the titles of books recently published from a study led by my colleague, Professor Nelle Slater.[1] Will our discipleship constitute responsible citizenship just because it is faithful? That is what all other Americans wonder. But will our freedom to be faithful disciples be respected? That is what we wonder. And, of course, we wonder among ourselves what constitutes the Bible's authority that we may be faithful disciples in ways recommended by its witness.

It is this conversation among ourselves—our uncertainties and overcertainties, our disagreements and their implications for what policies we will publicly advocate—that is of immense interest to all other Americans. The kind of authority the Bible is considered to have and the way in which it is interpreted influence not only the message we preach but also the politics we espouse.

I need not document this claim here; the prominent role played in the elections of 1980 and 1984 by conservative evangelical Christians and even by fundamentalist Christians makes the point when compared with the role of liberal Christians.[2] In this connection two things need to be noticed. The ways in which politics will differ among fundamentalist, conservative, and liberal Christians (what would a "moderate" Christian look like?), are not completely predictable. And it took this surge into politics to get liberal Christians' attention to the *theology* of conservative and fundamentalist evangelicals. It is this theology, especially as it treats biblical authority, that is of significant interest to all American citizens. The implications for public policy issues, I will suggest, have to do with this interest.

A brief look backward to two contemporary but disparate Christians may serve to show what I have in mind here. During the autumn term of 1903 the first president of the University of Chicago, William Rainey Harper, was disturbed by what he heard in the convocation lecture by Professor George Burman Foster of the Divinity School. The reputation of his school among Baptists of the Midwest was on President Harper's mind. He did not think Foster's talk, "The Ethics of Doctrinal Reform," helped this reputation any. As he feared, word got out in the church press and in the public press, and controversy erupted. Harper thought these were unpromising places to air theological differences. A great Bible scholar and promoter of biblical knowledge in his own right, Harper supported Foster and may have shared many of his views. But the upshot of the ensuing controversy was Foster's transfer from theology in the Divinity School to philosophy of religion in the University in the spring of 1905.

At this time, in the autumn of 1904, a woman evangelist by the name of Maria Woodworth-Etter conducted a revival meeting in Indianapolis. She was hitting her stride after almost twenty-five years as an itinerant preacher in whose meetings she and others would be thrown to the floor, gripped by a trance. Healings were claimed, and perhaps known and unknown tongues spoken. Later in 1914 Maria Woodworth-Etter would found a tabernacle in Indianapolis and make this city her home and point of departure. But her biographer reports that a veil of silence covers her from 1905 to 1912, the period in which the remarkable revival on Azusa Street in Los Angeles accelerated the emergence of the classical Pentecostal churches.[3]

It is significant, I think, that the biographer of Maria Woodworth-Etter was able to utilize along with her many published accounts of her ministry an extensive newspaper coverage of her revivals all over the country. Always accompanied by controversy, the merits and demerits of her ministry were reported and debated by reporters and editors in the daily papers. Her campaign in St. Louis earlier in 1904 resulted in the loss of her ordination in the Winebrennerian Churches of God. The Indianapolis Star reported that Maria's meetings in 1904 drove persons insane.[4] But generally she welcomed the newspaper publicity and depended upon it to create interest in her meetings, which it did.

This was not the case with President Harper at the University of Chicago. At the peak of the controversy over Professor Foster in 1905, Harper, who had suffered two serious operations and within a year would succumb to a cancer the university sought to conceal from the public, bared his soul to his doctor:

> I am disgusted with American journalism. Nothing is rightly interpreted; everything is presented in the wrong light. I wonder sometimes whether it is worthwhile to try to set things right.[5]

With respect to our differences about biblical authority, I suggest it may well be worthwhile to set things right as a matter of the church's public policy.

The reason is that whether we are preaching the gospel that men and women can be converted and transformed, or whether we are debating biblical authority in our seminaries, or whether we are acting politically to transform the structure of our society, we are acting in a public world. We cannot escape our embodiment as social creatures. However other persons may dispose themselves toward the preaching and political action of the churches, they also have an intrinsic interest in what we say among ourselves. That is why they take pains to "eavesdrop" on our churchly debates and report them in the papers. The premise of my remarks here is that the public has a vested interest in the faithfulness of our discipleship and the theology in terms of which we define and interpret it.

Accordingly, I will do two things in this concluding essay. I will discuss the implications of biblical authority for public policy issues in terms of four theses that will be stated and elaborated. Then I will offer a possible way of accounting for our differences about biblical authority that is informed by insights from the philosophy of art. My mood as I undertake this is irenic but critical and constructive. By utilizing insights from aesthetic criticism I think I will be saying things able to be appreciated by Professors Johnson and Placher. At the same time I am drawn to the kind of semantic concerns expressed by Professors Cottrell and Scholer that require to be addressed. Though he was not thinking of conversation between liberals and conservatives but between revisionists and postliberals, Professor Placher expresses my perspective when he wrote in his most recent book, "We have to think about how to set public policy in the midst of *genuine* pluralism...."[6]

I turn now to four theses about the implications of biblical authority for public policy.

Thesis One: The churches and individual Christians will press for public policies the warrants for which they derive from the Bible. Stated in a more nuanced way, the Bible will be influential in public policy debates, as it has in the past, both as directly proposing models (e.g., theocratic) and as indirectly supporting some models (e.g., democratic). A large literature has emerged, especially since the celebration of our nation's bicentennial, showing the way models vary with the way biblical authority is construed.[7] Scholars continue to debate the gnarled question of the relation of what Sidney Mead called the "religion of the Republic" and Robert Bellah called "civil religion" to the religion of the "churches"—Protestant, Jewish, Roman Catholic.[8] Mead claimed the evangelical community by the mid-nineteenth century learned to combine its discipleship with its citizenship harmoniously.[9] The strenuous effort of the courts to balance First Amendment rights to freedom of religion with its prohibition of the establishment of religion testifies to the Republic's fidelity to its side of the bargain. Events in the twentieth century, however, have shown both the churches and the Republic's other citizens have become wary of each other.[10] Ours had definitely become a polarizing political style that characterizes decision-making not only in our legislatures but also in our churches.[11] While this provides appropriate drama in the courtroom and appeals to the media's nose for sensationalism, it is subversive of trust that is essential to any community that values justice, truth, and peace.

But my concern here is constructive rather than historical. How can we hear ourselves debate about public policies concerning such issues as women's procreative freedom, nuclear disarmament, capital punishment, sanctuary for political refugees whatever their politics, pornography, the economic order? But we find it hard, also, to hear each other clearly when we speak of the place of the Bible in public discourse. A fascinating debate that shows this broke out in the pages of *The Christian Century* in the spring of 1986. A Presbyterian minister from New Jersey published an article titled, "The Bible and Public Policy."[12] At the end of the debate he summed up his views:

> I did not suggest in my article that the church plays no role in public-policy discussion or that the Bible should not inform the church's understanding of its role....But

we must distinguish between the church's role in public policy and the *Bible's* role in public policy. The Bible has authority over the church, the community of faith, not over the United States, a pluralistic society whose authoritative "scripture" remains the Constitution.[13]

Jeffrey Siker here reiterates the required distinctions overlooked in his article by his respondents, who were sophisticated and reputable clergypersons. We live in a messy world that requires that distinctions be made. Politics encourages us to harden distinctions into mutually exclusive alternatives. The positive point being made was that the only arguments we have a right to expect to be convincing in the public sphere are ethical ones, not theological ones. But the distinctions made by political polemics and slogans are usually clumsy, self-serving, and in any case unable to impose an antiseptic cleanness on the world—ethically or theologically. This is why trust must undergird our conversations.

Thesis Two: There will continue to be confusing diversity both in substantive proposals for public policy and in biblical warrants for them. This is implied in the first thesis and by the ambiguity of life alluded to. It is also implicated by our own sinful propensities. We may often benefit by equivocation, deliberate vagueness, and hidden agendas. This is evident, I think in debates about abortion policy and environmental protection. In the language of the sociology of knowledge, a public policy creates a "plausibility structure" supporting biblical authority when it conforms to biblical mandates as these are interpreted. The prevention of women's access to abortion serves this interest and may stand in the way of a more balanced consideration of the ethical and constitutional issues. Likewise, failure to address hard questions about the ethics of chemical and nuclear pollution of the environment with their disturbance of our millennia-long achievement of symbiosis may be due in part to reluctance to acknowledge the role of evolution. In these ways a view of biblical authority combined with interpretation has a significant impact upon debates about public policy. We should also be attentive to the way others can exploit ambiguity and employ it against us. We need to ask who benefits from the prolongation of debate, the proliferation of controversies, the provision of impediments to consensus and action. This thesis requires us to search our hearts for evidence of an impaired self-awareness in our discipleship and citizenship.

Thesis Three: As churches and individual Christians make their voices heard in public policy debates, we should accept responsibility to educate the public about the nature and significance of our theological differences. We cannot undertake this responsibly, of course, if we are self-deceived about our interests and unclear about how we warrant our proposals theologically and the substantive implications of that. This required self-awareness and rational clarity means there is an ethical dimension to our intramural conversations as well as our extramural politicking. To the degree that we are disingenuous and dissimulate in our relationships with one another for the sake of a political victory (in the church or in the public sphere), we risk becoming unethical and even ruthless. It is wholly possible to advocate what is morally right in a way that is morally wrong. But if we undertake to inform the public about why we differ, we will not be able to get away with this, since the language of ethics and moral responsibility is the language of the public sphere. But whether we do or not, the public "eavesdrops" on us. They know what is going on. For example, hypocrisy is not tolerated in the churches as the fate of two television evangelists recently shows. Against our own self-interest, then, this thesis urges the churches to interpret our differences to the public, offering especial help to reporters, journalists, and politicians, who indeed are our spokespersons and representatives in the public sphere.

Thesis Four: The Bible proposes a vision for all human life, received by Jews and Christians, and it does so with an authority all Christians regard as in some sense divine. The Bible proposes this vision as a "text," the literary document that it is with its diversity of genre. Consequently, it makes this proposal in a complicated way. I think all the speakers at this conference will agree with this thesis, though Professor Placher might have reservations about my reference to *all* human life. But I have anticipated this by the modifying phrase "received by Jews and Christians." Some theologians speak of the Bible as "divine." But I do not take them to mean the Bible is God, though I am not sure of the logic and semantics of their affirmation of the divinity of the Bible. In any case, I am satisfied no Christians, however strong their convictions about biblical authority and the way they press their claims, intend to be bibliolaters.[14] I think, also, that all the speakers at this conference would agree that the Bible's authority finds its "voice" not only in the letter of the book but also in the witness of Christians in and out of the churches.

These four theses suggest the complexity of the way the Bible's authority impacts the matter of shaping public policy in a constitutional republic such as ours. The proposal I make as I conclude my address does not claim to dispel this complexity. It seeks only to interpret this complexity in a way that respects God's use of the Bible as a means of grace in the redemption of the world and that accounts for the unity of the body of Christ despite our diverse interpretations. As for the public conduct of citizens who are not Christians, the complexity of the way the Bible has authority requires them to hear biblical appeals respectfully and in the right way, that is, as non-coercive proposals to them that have been persuasive to us. As for the public conduct of citizens like us who are Christians, the complexity of the way the Constitution effects the rule of law requires us to accept ethical responsibility for the way we dispose ourselves as disciples toward constitutional protections of freedom. As citizens and disciples we cannot escape these two complexities: the authority of the Bible and the Constitution.

I will now attempt a constructive theological proposal that attends to further complexity in the way the biblical text carries authority. The purpose is not to overcome the complexity (and consequent mystery to reason), which cannot be overcome. The purpose is to give an account of why theological construals differ. To the degree the account succeeds, I hope Christians will be more charitable to those who differ from them and more responsible in their discipleship and citizenship. Nor is this account expected to persuade persons to alter their theologies. It does, however, claim to illuminate the way the church enjoys unity with diversity.

This proposal utilizes the intrinsically aesthetic structure of the way the Bible has authority within our experience of the world. This experience can be said to have a basically aesthetic quality because persons have bodies and their worlds are apprehended not only with form but also with feeling. Experience is perceptual, combining sensation, emotion, imagination, and thinking. The world is experienced both as given to us and as influenced by us. A feature of our minds is that we can think of ourselves in what Edmund Husserl called "the natural standpoint" and go about living our lives as well as we can within it. Within this standpoint we can wonder whether the world is only of our making subjectively. Or we can wonder whether it is only objectively given. And we can doubt, as Renee Descartes did, one or the other, or both—that is, that we exist to know or that there is anything to know. And when we may be unable to distinguish any boundary between a real and an unreal world or between ourselves and what is not ourselves, then we may need more help than a philosopher can give us and call upon a psychiatrist. Of course, neither has the power to help us with the consent of our freedom, which is a large part of what it is to be embodied spirit. All this takes place within the natural standpoint. But we can also suspend the natural standpoint by an imaginative act of the mind that Husserl called an *epoche,* and pay attention only to *what* appears to us when the world appears to us.[15] This is to set aside questions about its reality or unreality, whether it is made up by us or given to us, whether it is "out there" or "in here." Attention is paid only to its qualities as it is presented to the mind's awareness. This object, which Husserl called an "essence," is simply what it is as a whole or gestalt with its qualities. This object perceived as a whole with its qualities is what is called an "aesthetic object."

I will say more about this presently, but I am concerned now only to identify it and to remind you that the aesthetic object is present in the world of the natural standpoint, not outside of it. Thereby it is not unreal. It is apprehended by a movement of the mind that discloses it, for amid the preoccupations of our lives in the natural standpoint it can be overlooked. It is called *aesthetic* because it is perceived with its own unity and structure and with its own feeling tones. It is not called a concept despite its presentation in mental space and time consciousness. It is called an *object* because it is not an abstraction but is perceived whole with qualities communicating with feelings. It may be beautiful or ugly in virtue of its structural elements. It may be pleasurable or repulsive. But I will not be dealing with these aspects of aesthetics. In what I have remaining to say I will show how the aesthetic structure of biblical authority is implicated in our conversations and then how that structure supports the biblical witness to the truth of God.

Professor Placher quite properly objects to the quantification of biblical authority implied by distinctions among conservative, moderate, and liberal views. He says this sets us against each other and proposes a different kind of classification. Our conference schema permits the authoritative-propositions model to constrict our vision of the real complexity of the Bible's authority. By proposing the transforming-word and narration-of God's-identity models in addition, he sets our vision free to grasp the complexity of our situation, which includes our unity despite our differences. This is an act of framing that suspends the natural standpoint (our disagreements about what is or is not true about the Bible and the world), and proposes alternative frames or models for consideration. It is also a constructive theological act of framing proposed within the natural standpoint in which the concerns of each model have their proper place. These mental moves derive from the recursive or reflexive structure of consciousness.[16]

Professor Johnson's essay suggests that he finds both the transforming-word and narration-of-God's identity models informative for the question of the Bible's authority. Here he finds the Greek Testament "most deserving of the designation *inerrant*" (p. 95). He means, I take it, that its witness to our freedom to be transformed as persons according to the mind of Christ who identifies God is true. Professor Cottrell calls this kind of view (rightly, I think) a functional or existential view. But he considers it inadequate because the truth of *everything* the Bible asserts must be true, for it is truth as such that enjoys the authority to compel belief (pp. 23f.). This "internal" authority is in some tension with the "external" and personal authority that is Godself. But the plenary and verbal inerrancy claimed for the Bible keeps God honest in Cottrell's view and I can only applaud that. God does not transform and save us by means of lies, whatever the divine right to do so. But I applaud even louder when Cottrell says,

> The Bible's truth (and therefore authority) is not its only appeal to humankind. Especially, the truth of the Gospel has a non-cognitive appeal as well; it draws us emotionally and aesthetically and existentially as well as intellectually (p. 37).[17]

I do not intend to tell Professor Cottrell what he thinks, but what he says here about the gospel and God's integrity is very close to what I mean by an aesthetic object or image in which we see our life in relation to God—in the natural standpoint! I (and, I think, Professor Placher) am speaking about biblical authority with a suspension of the natural standpoint. Cottrell, unlike Placher and me, does not make this move that treats the gospel within a larger frame as an aesthetic object negotiated within the natural standpoint. Consequently, the aesthetic and emotional appeal of the gospel is considered non-cognitively. But I consider it to have cognitive significance, albeit of a complex and fragile kind, within the natural standpoint. The aesthetic object, for example, differs for every person. The divine authority is found in *it*, not in the text as text or as propositions encoded in the text. The biblical text contributes its meaning decisively to the aesthetic object, but not in a way that requires plenary verbal inerrancy. The Bible's authority resides in its respect in the community of faith and God's use of it there as a means of grace. Its cognitive significance is found in this use. I will presently try to account for this cognitive significance.

Professor Scholer also seeks to preserve the veracity of the biblical text as the locus of meaning, which imposes "significant controls." Perhaps in a way not countenanced by Cottrell, however, in an article published in 1988, he acknowledged that its meaning is found in the "inextricable interplay" of text and interpreter creating "a hermeneutical reality and predicament from which there is no escape."[18] To preserve the text's control of the meaning, its "interpretive center" must be found in Jesus and the Greek Testament. But he acknowledges other claimed centers may derive from "an interpreter selected biblical-theological grid" that he says "controls" the meaning.[19] This meaning sounds very much like the aesthetic object I am seeking to identify, but without the Bible's authority and its witness included. It is still interpreter pitted against the text, instead of the two embraced within the "inextricable interplay" that takes place in the real world where the Bible is authoritative for him. As I regard it, the aesthetic object is produced in the "space" of this interplay and includes the internal witness of the Holy Spirit.

I refer to my conference colleagues in these ways to show that their analyses confirm the aesthetic dynamics of the Bible's authority. In addition to the agreement that the Bible is authoritative, I think it may be said agreement prevails about the following points also. 1. The meaning of the Bible's authority as well as if its text is complex and difficult to define. 2. The biblical text is an artifact that is historically conditioned, a literary document of many genres. 3. Not the Bible as "sacred object" (Johnson, p. 88), but the meaning-impregnated text as interpreted is the center of the authority issue. 4. The Bible's interpreters are also historically conditioned. 5. The Bible speaks for and bears witness to "an Other" (Johnson, p. 90) who is God. 6. The Bible's truth, the truth of its truth-claims, is part of its authority. As I seek now to give an account of our agreement and differences by reference to the phenomenon of an aesthetic object, I am especially mindful of Professor Cottrell's stress on this last item of our agreement, the Bible's truth-telling.

We have observed that aesthetic objects emerge in experience unselfconsciously but then must be attended by a suspension of the natural attitude. Our respect and use of the Bible can be said to involve an aesthetic object (or image, to employ a visual metaphor) created by the interplay of text and interpreter. The text brings its encoded meaning. The interpreter brings his or her beliefs of all kinds. It all transpires in the real world and the aesthetic object is created a phenomenal object there that is no less real for its phenomenal quality.[20] Henry David Aiken has shown that many kinds of beliefs—natural, cultural, aesthetic—play indispensable roles in the creation and appreciation of works of art.[21] There are, he says, behavioral and mental aspects of beliefs. "On their behavioral side, beliefs are perhaps best conceived as expectancies or ideo-motor sets which dispose us to act when, as and if something is the case." On the mental side they are "feelings of acceptance."[22] To distinguish play and enter a game involves what Aiken calls a "generic aesthetic belief," which is a framing or setting apart as a whole that we have called bracketing or suspending the natural standpoint. It has the effect of displacing other beliefs (in some degree at least) and preventing them "from issuing forth into the overt behavior which would convert the response into practical activity.[23] The witness of the Bible in general and of Jesus' parables invite us to consider an aesthetic object called the rule (kingdom) of God. Christians try to play this "game" in the world. But is it just a game? Are the boundaries of its playing field so distinct after all?

Roman Ingarden also speaks of the ways belief is ingredient in an aesthetic object, which emerges with the perception of a real object such as a "work of art," an experience in nature, or a book. In Ingarden's special sense of a work of art, not as "an artifact considered with respect to its design,"[24] the gospel or the rule of God can be considered God's works of art "fixed" by the Bible and Jesus' teaching, and even the preacher's sermon.[25] In Ingarden's terms we can say that the gospel and the rule of God are always made concrete in the encounter of an interpreter with the text. "Empirically a work is always manifested to an observer in some concretion."[26] This concretion is the aesthetic object emergent in a composite and phased temporal process in which it presents itself as the whole that it is and appreciated for its intrinsic value only, "something *contained in the object itself* and based on the qualities and the harmony of the qualities of the aesthetic object itself."[27] This is no mere abstraction gathering particulars in a concept, this is aesthetic object. It is concrete, qualitied, with feeling borne by meaning accompanied by emotion.

After an initial, primarily emotional phase of impact by some quality in this aesthetic experience, Ingarden speaks of "various moments of the nature of a conviction." Some of them are *"akin* to those which occur in cognitive experiences (and particularly in perceptive ones) and related to real objects."[28] There are three such moments.

1. There is the conviction of the existence of the object in its givenness that presupposes the general *conviction of the existence* of the real world that we live in and entertain in the natural attitude. The similarity of the presentation of this object to the presentation of perceived objects in the natural world is, as it were, so marked that the conviction of its existence causes the "dampening" or "neutralizing" (Husserl) of the difference it represents from ordinary perception. The effect of this is so great, Ingarden says, "we behave as if we *feigned* such a conviction."[29] This way of putting it is faithful to the dialectical complexity of our belief in the rule of God and the gospel, for we *behave* as if our conviction were not feigned. This is clearly not to play at the kingdom of God.

2. There is also a "conviction-moment concerning the *whole* aesthetic object as a *harmony of qualities.*"[30] This is a belief

about the value and quality of the gospel or rule of God (the works of God presented in the aesthetic object) that accounts for the persuasive authority and power of the feeling born by meaning fixed by the text.

3. There is also the conviction that since *there is* something of this kind, there is the possibility that the real world itself or objects in the real world with these qualities exist. Thereby we may really believe the Bible witnesses truthfully. Ingarden says, however, that this moment of conviction is "absolutely independent of the conviction of the reality of the surrounding real world."[31] By this he means that this conviction is mediated by an aesthetic object, not by a concept. It allows no formal deductions yielding sound conclusions to arguments about physical objects in the natural world, for example, the truth of statements made in the Bible. Yet it may have practical conclusions of large empirical significance.

This is not to be taken as a refutation of anyone else's account of the authority of the Bible. It is more a rendering of an account of my belief in the Bible's authority. It is important to appreciate that differences about public policies warranted by the Bible can depend upon different ways of construing the Bible's authority. In turn, different construals of biblical authority may well depend upon whether or not the level of mental recursion that attends to the aesthetic object produced in biblical reading and interpretation is reached. The nature of the Bible's inerrancy claimed by fundamentalists, for example, seems to turn on this matter. Perhaps differences between conservatives and liberal interpreters that seem so intractable may be accounted for by differences in recursive levels acknowledged in their work. Perhaps, too, this can help us appreciate how the grace of the Holy Spirit creates and preserves our unity despite our interpretive differences.

Since I have offered a theological construal, it may be appropriate to conclude with reference again to President William Rainey Harper of the University of Chicago. In response to a Disciples minister at Nevada, Missouri, who inquired about the liberal "New Theology" and its impact on Harper's missionary zeal, Harper responded in 1905:

134

Personally I can honestly say that my missionary zeal
has suffered no diminution whatever on account of
my change in theological views. On the contrary, I
think I am now more interested in the propagation of
truth than I ever have been before....You will really
understand, of course, that all my work is in a very
fundamental sense missionary work....

I am quite sure that the New Theology will not be
"effective in really saving men from their sins," because no theology has ever saved any man from his
sins. Theology is, of course, only a human philosophical interpretation in certain facts in religious
experience and it must always be the experience that
brings salvation, not the interpretation of the experience.[32]

Harper is right about the shortcomings of theology, of
course, though his view of theology has its own shortcomings. And has he undone everything I have said? Or maybe
he just wasn't saved. But that's another story.

NOTES

[1]Nelle G. Slater, ed., *Tensions Between Citizenship and Discipleship: A Case Study* (New York: Pilgrim Press, 1989) and Mary C. Boys, ed., *Education for Citizenship and Discipleship* (New York: Pilgrim Press, 1989).
[2]Cf. Richard Pierard and James L. Wright, "The Moral Majority in Indiana" in David Bromley and Anson Shupe, eds., *New Christian Politics* (Macon: Mercer University Press, 1984), pp. 195-212; and Richard Pierard, "Reagan and the Evangelicals" in Marla Selvidge, ed., *Fundamentalism Today: What Makes It So Attractive?* (Elgin: The Brethren Press, 1984), pp. 47-61.
[3]Wayne E. Warner, *The Woman Evangelist: The Life and Times of Charismatic Evangelist Marie B. Woodworth-Etter* (Metuchen: The Scarecrow Press, 1986), pp. 161-163 and Chapter 11.
[4]*Ibid.*, p. 184, n. 13; p. 185, n. 19.
[5]William Rainey Harper to Dr. Nicholas Senn, June 1, 1905. (University of Chicago Archives/Presidents' Papers, Box 49, folder 4.) I have discussed the matter of Foster in "A 'Singleminded' Theologican: George Burman Foster at Chicago," *Foundations* 20 (1977), pp. 36-59, 163-180.

[6]William C. Placher, *Unapologetic Theology: A Christian Voice in a Pluralistic Conversation* (Louisville: Westminster/John Knox Press, 1989), p. 168.

[7]Cf. Nathan O. Hatch and Mark A. Noll, eds., *The Bible in America: Essays in Cultural History* (New York: Oxford University Press, 1982).

[8]Cf. Sidney E. Mead, *The Lively Experiment: The Shaping of Christianity in America* (New York: Harper and Row, 1963); Will Herberg, *Protestant-Catholic-Jew: An Essay in American Religious Sociology* (Garden City: Doubleday, 1955); Robert Bellah, *Beyond Belief: Essays on Religion in a Post-Traditional World* (New York: Harper and Row, 1970); and the work of John F. Wilson. Recently, pentecostal, charismatic and black churches have been considered a "third force" in christendom in works by Winthrop Hudson and William McLaughlin.

[9]Cf. Sidney E. Mead, *The Nation with the Soul of a Church* (New York: Harper and Row, 1975), chapter 1.

[10]Cf. U.S. Commission on Civil Rights, *Religion in the Constitution: A Delicate Balance* (Washington, D.C., 1983) and John T. Noonan, Jr., *The Believer and the Powers that Are: Cases, History and Other Data Bearing on the Relation of Religion and Government* (New York: Macmillan Publishing Co., 1987).

[11]People of the American Way was organized by Normal Lear to counterbalance Jerry Falwell's Moral Majority.

[12]Jeffrey S. Siker, "The Bible and Public Policy," *The Christian Century* 103 (1986), pp. 171-173, and "The Bible's Role in Public Affairs" (Readers' Response), *ibid.*, pp. 389-394.

[13]Jeffrey S. Siker, Church's Public Role (Letter), *ibid.*, p. 564.

[14] Cf. Edgar A. Towne, "Fundamentalism's Theological Challenge to the Churches," in Maria Selvidge, ed., *op.cit.*, pp. 31-45.

[15]The interests not only of philosophers of art and theologians converge here, but also of philosophers of mind and psychotherapists.

[16]Cf. Hilary Lawson, *Reflexivity: The Post-modern Predicament* (LaSalle: Open Court, 1985).

[17]I ascribe some cognitive significance to the aesthetic object. There is an assurance that we know but not a knowing that we know. Cf. Jack W. Cottrell, "Dedicated to Scriptural Inerrancy—The Biblical/Theological Implications," *The Seminary Review* 30 (1984), pp 93-107, and "Inerrancy as a Restoration Principle," *ibid.*, 34 (1988), pp. 89-105.

[18]David M. Scholer, "Issues in Biblical Interpretation," *The Evangelical Quarterly* 60 (1988), pp. 11, 13.

[19]*Ibid.*, pp. 16f.

[20]Gregory Bateson and Lonnie Kliever, among others, use the playing of games to analyze this capacity to bracket the natural standpoint. Fiction and reality are also contrasted. This is useful so long as it is clear that the distinctions involved presuppose a standpoint occupied outside the game or story by which they are known indubitably to be playful and fictive.

[21]Henry David Aiken, "The Aesthetic Relevance of Belief." *The Journal of Aesthetics and Art Criticism* 9 (1951), pp. 301-315.

[22]*Ibid.*, p. 305.

[23]*Ibid.*, p. 311.

[24]The definition of Joseph Margolis, *The Language of Art and Art Criticism* (Detroit: Wayne State University Press, 1965), p. 44.

[25]Roman Ingarden, "Artistic and Aesthetic Values," *The British Journal of Aesthetics* 4 (1964), 198-213.

[26]*Ibid.*, p. 199.

[27]Roman Ingarden, "Aesthetic Experience and Aesthetic Object," in Nathaniel Lawrence and Daniel O'Conner, eds., *Readings in Existential Phenomenology* (Englewood Cliffs: Prentice-Hall, 1967), p. 320.

[28]*Ibid.*, p. 332.

[29]*Ibid.*, p. 312.

[30]*Ibid.*, p. 322.

[31]*Ibid.*, pp. 322f.

[32]William Rainey Harper to Rev. G.D. Edwards, February 11, 1905. (University of Chicago Archives/William Rainey Harper Papers, VII, 19.)

Printed in the United States
19845LVS00001B/418-456